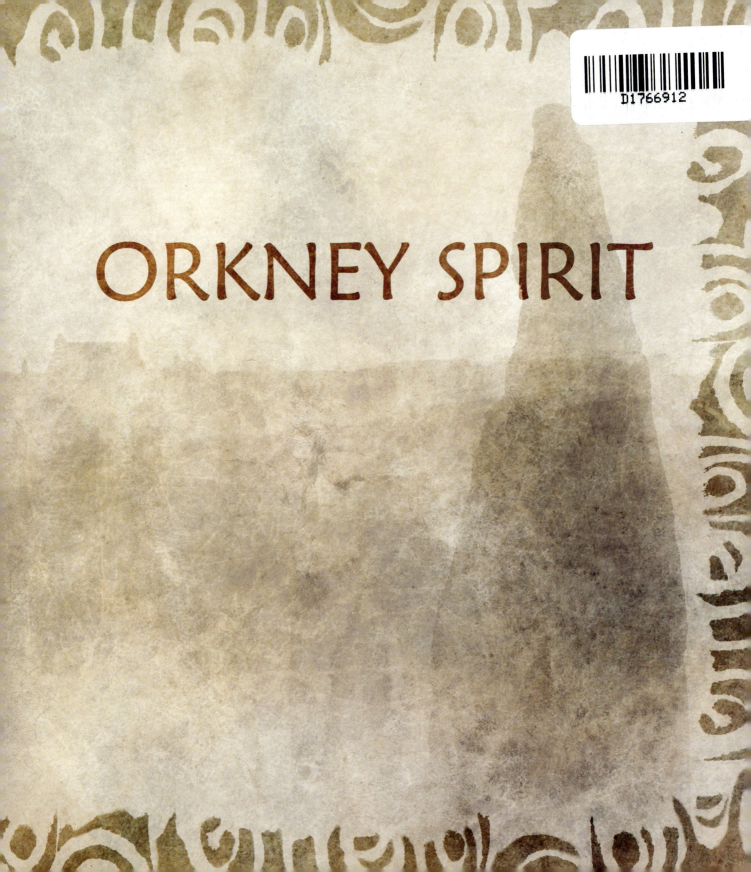

ORKNEY SPIRIT

ORKNEY SPIRIT

Liz Ashworth

Artwork and Design by Selena S.Kuzman

SANDSTONEPRESS
HIGHLAND | SCOTLAND

'He that is of a cheerful heart hath
a continual feast.' – NKJV Proverbs Ch 15, V15.

First published in Great Britain 2010
by Sandstone Press Ltd
PO Box 5725
One High Street
Dingwall
Ross-shire
IV15 9WJ
Scotland

www.sandstonepress.com

Editor: Robert Davidson

The publisher acknowledges subsidy from the Scottish Arts Council towards
the publication of this book.

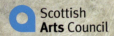

ISBN-13: 978-1-905207-32-9

Printed and bound in Poland

CONTENTS

Bustling kitchens filled with welcoming warmth, mouth watering aromas and bake day clutter are sadly disappearing. Have you ever been enticed by a newly baked scone, cooled just enough for a first bite oozing with home-made strawberry jam? Or piles of warm fresh-baked oat cakes that invite a chunk of cheese or smother of golden butter? Baking and cooking together is about giving, sharing, companionship and banter, not to mention wholesome home-made goodness.

From the age of four I loved to help in the kitchen - not perhaps to my mother's delight. She planted a love of cooking in my sister and me, which we both still remember and share. I am eternally grateful to her for this and pass it on wherever I can.

Although Orcadian blood flows through my veins my feet did not stand on Orkney's soil until later in life. On my first unforgettable flight to Kirkwall the plane soared over a colourful tapestry of farms, houses, cattle, sheep, and clear turquoise waters dappled with darting shoals of fish and popping heads of seals illuminated by the fire-lit backdrop of a golden setting sun.

It was more than a beginning or a welcome; I felt I had come home at last. The place that I love to be with family and friends; baking and cooking to my heart's content; joining in with community spirit; copious cups of tea, sometimes something stronger, and piles of amazing home bakes, music, laughter and 'yap'.

As they say in Orkney : Hoo's it goin. Come awa in.
It's good to see you. Come away into the kitchen.

This book is dedicated to the generous helping of family and friends, old and new, who loved, supported, read and tasted with great fortitude.

THE SKARA BRAE DELI

Before Stonehenge, before the pyramids, was Skara Brae. Situated on the Bay of Skaill in the North West of Orkney's mainland, Skara Brae's cluster of ten houses is Europe's most complete Neolithic Village. Now with World Heritage Site Status it is often referred to as 'Britain's Pompeii'. I wonder what those ancient settlers would feel if they could time travel to realise that they had 'Award Winning Deli' potential. The 'Skara Braes' knew a good thing when they arrived 5000 years ago.

The rich naturally fertile soil easily grew fantastic wheat and barley and with no food miles it was easy to support the local producer, indeed it was hard not to. This land of birch, hazel and willow scrub sheltered wild boar and deer for the hunting, and was filled with wild herbs and berries for the picking. The lochs, streams and sea swam with every sort of fish and the high cliffs covered with sea birds were great for fresh meat and eggs.

Could this have this amounted to the original, sustainable, organic farm deli?

Ready to use building materials were free at point of use; driftwood from the Americas regularly washed up on the beach among more than enough pebbles and stones to build with and, to top it all, a never ending supply of sea weed for fuel.

They were brave fishermen who ventured far from shore in their 'designer' boats, a cross between a canoe and a wooden raft, trapping oysters, crab and lobster, fishing for ling, haddock, cod, and hake, with the odd conger eel thrown in for good measure. Distant adventures added whale or shark, and if the weather was inclement there were always trout and, in season, salmon in the streams and lochs.

After all, nothing is new under the sun. Organic, traceable, affordable, fresh, huge variety, pure, wholesome, unprocessed, no carbon footprint and sustainable, Skara Brae Deli — a winner!

HOT SEARED NEWLY CAUGHT TROUT

The people of Skara Brae would have cooked freshly caught fish by laying it on stones heated in, or at, the side of the fire. To prepare their food they used a nifty, multiple use, stone gadget. It was like a smoothed pebble on one side but honed to a sharp cutting edge on the other. The smooth part sat secure in the palm of the hand to allow the working part to scoop, chop, and scrape at will. It was an efficient, safe cutting tool, perhaps we could do with a similar one today.

Very simple, the fresher the fish the better
Serves 4 people
Takes 20 minutes to prepare and cook
Cook on a barbecue, hob or grill

You will need:-

4 fresh cleaned and gutted whole trout. Wild brown trout are best but you can use rainbow or Arctic char.
Sea salt
Freshly ground black pepper
Fresh herbs, choose from parsley, lemon thyme, bay leaves, dill, tarragon, mint
Light olive or sunflower oil and kitchen towel

To make:-

1. Put on the barbecue or grill to heat on high. Alternatively a ridged griddle pan or thick bottomed frying pan can be heated on the cooker hob.
2. Wash the cavity of the fish in cold running water and, if necessary, remove the heads
3. Wash the herbs, chop together or make into four little bundles, tied with thread or fine string.
4. Lightly season each fish cavity with a little sea salt and freshly ground black pepper. Add the herbs, chopped or in bundles, and fold closed. Secure with a wooden cocktail stick or sew a few stitches to secure using a large needle and thick thread.
5. Take a sharp knife to make a few diagonal slashes into the flesh on each side of the fish. Then lay each prepared fish onto a large flat plate.
6. Using a thick piece of kitchen towel and taking care not to burn fingers, rub the cooking surface with a little oil. If using the grill line the grill pan first with foil, then oil the grid over the foil lined pan.
7. Lay the fish flat onto the hot cooking surface and leave to cook on high till crisp on the outside and the juices begin to flow. The time this takes will depend on the size and type of fish you have chosen to cook.

8. A safe way to turn over the fish is to use a spatula or fish slice in your right hand to ease underneath and a fork in your left to hold the half cooked fish steady while you lift and turn to cook the other side. Cooking the fish under a hot grill, you will see when the fish is ready to turn over using the same technique.

9. When crisp on both sides reduce to a low heat to make sure that the flesh is cooked inside. Use the point of a knife or skewer to test after two to three minutes or longer for a larger fish. The flesh will be opaque all the way through and the juices will run clear.

10. Serve hot with plenty salad.

SKARA BRAE SALAD

It is difficult to know precisely what fruit and vegetables would have been eaten at Skara Brae. It is only possible deduce the content of their diet by analysing the remains of the rubbish heap or midden. Because bone preserves better than vegetable matter there is little left of the latter. This is a 21st Century version of what may have been eaten, which was naturally local, freshly picked and in season.

To make:-

1. Take a large salad bowl and fill with a mixture of any of the following:-
Fresh green leaves in season, for example; rocket, radicchio, mizuna, cos, sweetheart, lollo rosa, spinach.
Finely grated cabbage, carrot, parsnip or celeriac
Watercress or mustard cress

2. Mix the vegetables together and then carefully toss with chopped fresh herbs like parsley, tarragon, mint, lemon thyme and chives.

3. Scatter the top of the bowl at the last minute with fresh berries – blueberries, cherries, cranberries, toasted hazelnuts and seeds.

4. We will never know if a dressing was made. However, mixing together runny honey with fresh cranberry or sour cherry juice and seasoning with some fresh chopped herbs like dill or tarragon makes a delicious sauce/relish seasoning to go with the fish and salad.

NEWLY WEDS 1944 IN STYLE

My uncle the Rev. Stuart McAlpine and Aunt Eileen began their ministry and married life on the Orkney island of North Ronaldsay. All their worldly goods, packed into vast trunks and suitcases, were transported from Aberdeen on the MV St Rognvald to Kirkwall and there loaded onto the steamer Earl Sigurd for the crossing to the North Isles. To ferry their goods across the harbour at North Ronaldsay they engaged the services of the island lighter, a yole and its owner, rowing the dozen or so trips required to take the newly weds and all they possessed over to the jetty. Large trunks were filled with bed linen, crockery, pots, pans, cutlery and Uncle Stuart's treasured fiddle; settees, chairs, beds, all but the kitchen sink and large range that were already installed in the waiting manse.

Next day Uncle Stuart ventured out to meet his new parishioners while Aunt Eileen set about more mundane domestic arrangements. She was of the firm belief that a manse should hold an open door for all. So, getting her priorities in order she decided that sustenance came first. With her hair scrunched into an old headscarf tied in a turban, old gloves on, she attacked the grimy black leaded cooking range, 'gaean hid laldie' with a brillo and hot water, only to be caught unawares when her handsome new husband returned with a very glamorous lady parishioner whom he had invited for afternoon tea and home bakes.

NEWLY WEDS 1944 IN STYLE

Aunt Eileen was a great one for a 'wee samich'. No matter when you arrived, the kettle went on and like magic, sandwiches would appear. Wonderful, never to be repeated, concoctions slapped between two slices of hearty home-made loaf, served crusts and all. Affectionately known in some areas as 'a dimpit piece'.

MANSE MEAT PASTE

Makes enough for a large loaf of sandwiches.
A labour saving sandwich mix. Mix once, spread once.
No cooking required.

You will need:-
1 tin 350g (12ozs) corned beef,
chopped pork or similar
Margarine or butter
HP Sauce or Worcester sauce
Chutney

Any or all of the following:-
Chopped tomato, spring onion, chives.
Grated carrot, apple or handful of dried fruit
Curry powder for the adventurous

To make:-
1. Mince the meat through a Spong, chop in a food processor or mix to a paste in the bowl of an electric mixer using the K beater.
2. Beat in a generous dollop of soft margarine or butter then add some chutney or HP sauce to taste. For those who like spicy food try adding curry powder or paste along with a spoon or two of mango chutney. Invent as you go.
3. To make the meat go a bit further, include some of the suggested additions. Grated apple and a handful of raisins go well with the curry theme while an HP sauce mix is tasty with chopped tomato and spring onion.
4. Spread once, sandwich, cut and serve. Manse meat paste keeps in the fridge up to three days. Deep freeze up to two months.

POTTED CHEESE

A spread, filling, stir-in for rice and pasta, topping for grills, best on hot tattie scones.

You will need:-
About 225g (8ozs) grated bits of left over cheese
1 dessert spoon mustard – English, Dijon, Wholegrain
60g (2ozs) softened butter
Sea Salt
Freshly Ground Black Pepper

To make:-
1. Beat the ingredients together in a bowl. Season to taste, adding yoghurt or cream to make a spreading paste.
2. Store in a sealed container in the fridge up to two weeks or freeze no more than two months.

TATTIE SCONES

Makes enough for two rounds, or bannocks, which cut into 16 triangles or farls
Takes ten minutes to mix and bake
Bake on a flat griddle or
thick bottomed frying pan.

You will need:-
225g (8ozs) cooked potato
60g (2ozs) plain flour or fine oatmeal
0.5 teaspoon Baking Powder
15g (0.5oz) melted butter or margarine
Sea Salt

To make:-
1. Turn on the girdle or frying pan on medium heat.
2. Mash the potatoes with the butter and a little salt. Add a drop or two of milk if the potatoes are very dry.
3. Sift the flour and baking powder together.
4. Using your hands in a kneading action work in sufficient flour to make a smooth pliable dough.
5. Flour your hands, divide the dough into two halves shaping each into a ball. Flatten the ball with the palm of your hand, roll and turn, repeating till the dough is thin enough.
6. Cut each round into 6 or 8 triangles (known as farls).
7. Test the heat of the girdle or frying pan by shaking a little plain flour onto the surface. If it turns golden brown the heat is correct, too hot and it will burn. Shake off the flour and rub the hot surface with a little oil on kitchen towel.
8. Lay the scones on the girdle to bake for about three minutes on each side till golden.
9. Cool wrapped in a tea towel on a wire rack. Eat warm newly baked.

SERENADING SEALS

On arriving at the manse among the first items to be unpacked and given a place of honour was the McAlpine fiddle. Uncle Stuart never missed an opportunity to play. He also loved North Ronaldsay, his new island home, the sheer peace and remoteness, the stark beauty and being at one with nature. He would wander the rugged shores playing his fiddle to the rhythm of the roaring sea. The seals loved it and often answered back while the sheep just kept on doing what sheep do, and seabirds wheeled overhead.

Sometimes he would play a jig, or perhaps the odd reel or Strathspey. Did he compose as he played, meandering along the rocky shores? I will never know but I wish I could have been a buckie on a rock listening to that unique harmony.

SLOW ROASTED NORTH RONALDSAY MUTTON AND BLACK PUDDING STUFFING SERVED WITH A CHEESE AND ALE SAUCE

The range in the Manse kitchen was, and still is, ideal for slow cooking North Ronaldsay mutton. Over 60 years ago little would the Manse family have dreamt that such a local meat would be acclaimed internationally as a delicacy and served on the tables of the rich and famous. My chef friend, Paul Doull, has helped me to write a simplified version. Here it is in easy to follow steps.

SLOW ROASTED NORTH RONALDSAY MUTTON

Serves 6 to 8 people
Takes 7 hours to prepare,
slow roast and serve.
Oven Roast at 150C, 300F, Gas 2

You will need:-
2.5kg (5.5 lbs) North Ronaldsay Mutton on the bone
Sea salt
Ground black pepper
Fresh herbs, thyme, bay leaf, parsley, tied into a bundle

To make:-
1. Turn on the oven to heat making sure that the shelves are arranged to accommodate the roasting tin.
2. Season the meat with sea salt and freshly ground black pepper, add the herbs and double wrap with foil. Use thick turkey foil if you have any left in the cupboard.
3. Slow roast in the oven for four to five hours till the meat is literally falling off the bone. Turn down the oven after three hours to 140C, 275F, Gas 1.
4. Carve into thick slices and keep warm covered with foil.

BLACK PUDDING STUFFING

You will need:-
450G (1lb) black pudding
1 onion peeled and chopped
60g (2ozs) fresh bread crumbs
Sunflower oil

To make:-
1. Cook the onions slowly in a little oil till soft, stir in the black pudding and breadcrumbs.
2. Double wrap in foil and put into roast with the mutton for the last forty five minutes.
3. Alternatively steam in a covered basin for one hour.

CHEESE AND ALE SAUCE

Makes one pint of sauce.
Takes 15 minutes to make
Cook on the hob

You will need:-
60g (2ozs) margarine
60g (2ozs) plain flour
400mls (14 fl ozs) milk
200mls (7 fl ozs) Orkney pale ale
Sea salt
Ground black pepper

To make:-
1. Melt the margarine, stir in the flour and continue stirring to cook a little.
2. Remove from the heat and gradually add the milk and ale beating well. Use a balloon whisk to avoid lumps.
3. Return to the heat stirring all the time till the sauce thickens and boils.
4. Season to taste with sea salt and ground black pepper.

ORKNEY TATTIE AND SWEET POTATO MASH

Good to serve with this dish and easy to make.

Cook 1kg (2.2lbs) Orkney tatties (potatoes) with half that quantity of sweet potato in boiling salted water till tender.
If there is no sweet potato cook the tatties with turnip instead.
Drain and mash with a knob of butter till smooth. Taste and adjust seasoning if needed.

To serve:-
Serve on heated dinner or large soup plates.
Place a generous spoon of mash in the middle of the plate and arrange slices of mutton overlapping at the side along with a small spoon of stuffing.
Pour the sauce round the base and garnish with chopped mixed fresh herbs like parsley, chive and mint.

GREAT UNCLE HARRY'S BATH

The McAlpine home in North Ronaldsay Manse had, during the middle years of the 20ᵗʰ century, a private water supply. Fortunately, instead of dipping buckets into wells there was a slightly less laborious manual pump which provided water for day to day needs by the exercise of a few vigorous arm actions.

Bathing was a different matter. The large Victorian free standing bath filled with hot foaming water was a joyful experience but, to achieve this luxury, a certain amount of strategic planning was required. The tank had to be filled to overflowing to ensure a sufficient quantity of hot water.

First stoking the range in order to heat the necessary supply Uncle Stuart hand pumped until the over flow pipe did just that. A steady stream emerging indicated that the great bath time moment had arrived. This strategy provided a decent soak in shoulder depth hot water, one of his few relaxing indulgences.

A visit from the in-laws one summer proved an exception. One day during the visit Uncle Stuart decided that the great bath time moment had arrived so, with the stove well stoked and the water-heating fire roaring up the chimney, he set about pumping duties. Try as he might, pumping harder and harder, he just could not make that overflow drip appear. Aunt Eileen's brother Rory joined in the task but to no avail so, in the end, the pair gave up and cracked a bottle of home-brew instead.

Hardly had a drop passed their parched lips than Uncle Stuart's father-in-law, Great Uncle Harry, emerged glowingly scrubbed and sweetly smelling from a morning's bathing entertainment. 'By Jove, that's some bath', he extolled, 'and just gallons of hot water.' He had been drawing off the water as they pumped.

Staying on the Steamy Subject, may I suggest a Steam Pudding or Two?

ANGELS' TEARS

Named by Grandmother Ritchie to describe 'tears of jam' running down the sides of her 'heavenly' sponge. Using jams to hand your 'angels' may shed many a different tear; strawberry, raspberry, black currant, marmalade, a great favourite of my mother, or rhubarb and ginger to which I am rather partial.

Serves 4
Takes 15 minutes to mix
Steam on the hob for 1.5 hours
or cook three to five minutes in
the microwave

You will need:-
115g (4ozs) plain flour
45g (1.5ozs) margarine
2 level teaspoon baking powder
30g (1oz) sugar
1 large egg
Milk or water to mix
2 or 3 tablespoons of the jam of your choice

To make: -

1. Sieve the flour, baking powder and sugar into a bowl then rub in the fat.
2. Beat the egg and add to the mixture with enough water or milk to make a soft dropping consistency, like that of thick double cream.
3. Grease a pudding basin, spoon in the jam of your choice, top with the sponge mixture then cover with greaseproof paper securely tied with string or a thick rubber band.
4. Steam for at least 1 hour or, to save time, use a microwave.
5. To microwave: cover with cling-film pierced with the point of a knife or skewer, and cook on power level 700w to 800w for one minute intervals turning after each till risen and still slightly moist in the middle. Do not cook too long or you will end up with a brick! When using a microwave always remember that the food continues to cook after the processing time is complete.
6. Loosen the pudding with a flat bladed knife, place a warmed plate over the base, and holding the plate firm invert 180 degrees whereupon the pudding should slip from the pudding basin onto the plate. Scoop the warm jam on top to run down the sides in 'tears'. Serve with custard, cream or ice cream.

Cook's tip:-
Variety is the spice of life. Add either of these
A handful of sultanas and a spoon of honey or syrup instead of jam
Adding a teaspoon of ground ginger to the sponge mixture is a good match with rhubarb and ginger jam.

DARK TREACLE PUD – GRANDFATHER'S STYLE

My grandfather was the stalwart supporter of a spiced rich dark treacle pudding bursting with plump juicy raisins. This delicacy he sprinkled liberally with icing sugar which he affectionately referred to as 'Pol Sucroll!' Is this undiscovered Orcadian?

Serves 4 people
Takes 20 minutes to mix
Steam on the hob for 1.5 hours or cook in the microwave for 3 to 5 minutes

You will need: -
115g (4ozs) plain flour
45g (1.5ozs) margarine
2 teaspoons baking powder
1 level teaspoon mixed spice
60g (2ozs) raisins
1 egg, beaten
30g (1ozs) Black treacle
Milk or water to mix

To make:-
1. Sift the flour, baking powder and spice into a mixing bowl, add the margarine and rub in. Stir in the raisins and soft brown sugar.
2. Heat the treacle a little to mix in along with the egg and enough liquid to make a soft dropping consistency.
3. Turn into a greased pudding bowl, cover and steam for 1.5 hours till risen and firm. Make sure to check the water level to prevent the pan from boiling dry.
4. Alternatively cook in a microwave on power level 700w to 800 w. Cover with cling film and pierce with a sharp knife, or skewer, to allow steam to escape. Programme to bake for bursts of one minute, turning the bowl after each minute till risen and moist in the middle. Remove and allow cooking to complete.
5. Serve hot with Pol Sucroll (sifted icing sugar) and custard or cream.

Cook's tip:-
For a spicier pudding add 1 level teaspoon of ground ginger and a generous pinch of chilli powder.Mix in dried cranberries, sultanas or chopped dried apricots instead of raisins.

First Journey

Commenced Tuesday 19th February 1946. Ended Sunday 24th February.

Launceston

North Ronaldshay

By train to Aberdeen. By steamer St Rognvald to Kirkwall. Very stormy passage, taking 39 hours instead of 12. Delayed by gales in Kirkwall till Saturday 22nd February. Set out in Earl Sigurd but turned back after half an hour & returned to Kirkwall. Set out again Sunday 23rd Feb. in heavy snow. Arrived at North Ronaldshay after 4 hours sail. Deep snow. Very cold.

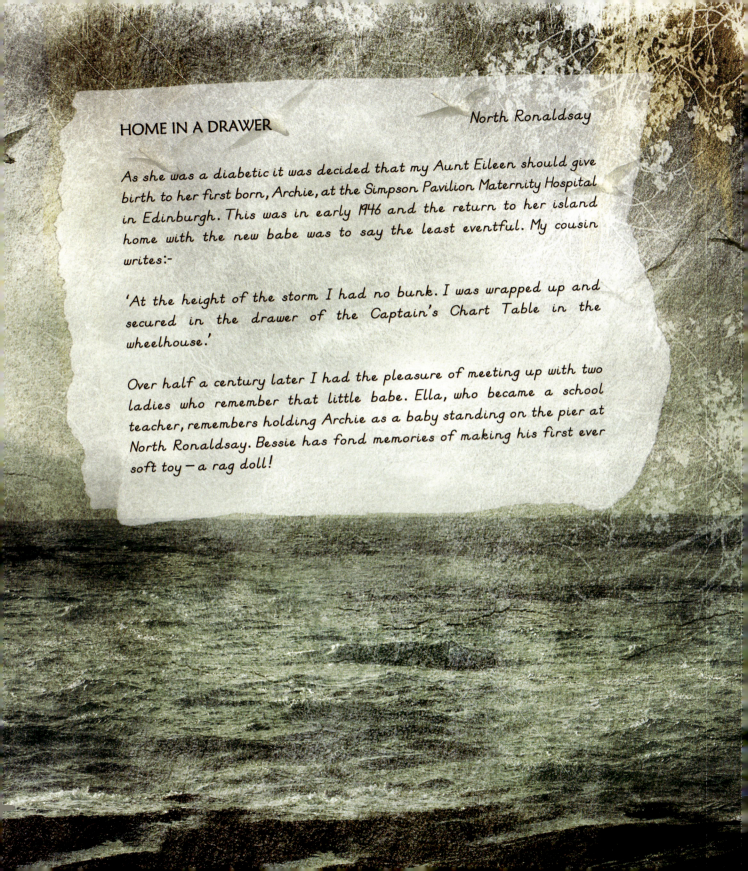

HOME IN A DRAWER

As she was a diabetic it was decided that my Aunt Eileen should give birth to her first born, Archie, at the Simpson Pavilion Maternity Hospital in Edinburgh. This was in early 1946 and the return to her island home with the new babe was to say the least eventful. My cousin writes:-

'At the height of the storm I had no bunk. I was wrapped up and secured in the drawer of the Captain's Chart Table in the wheelhouse.'

Over half a century later I had the pleasure of meeting up with two ladies who remember that little babe. Ella, who became a school teacher, remembers holding Archie as a baby standing on the pier at North Ronaldsay. Bessie has fond memories of making his first ever soft toy – a rag doll!

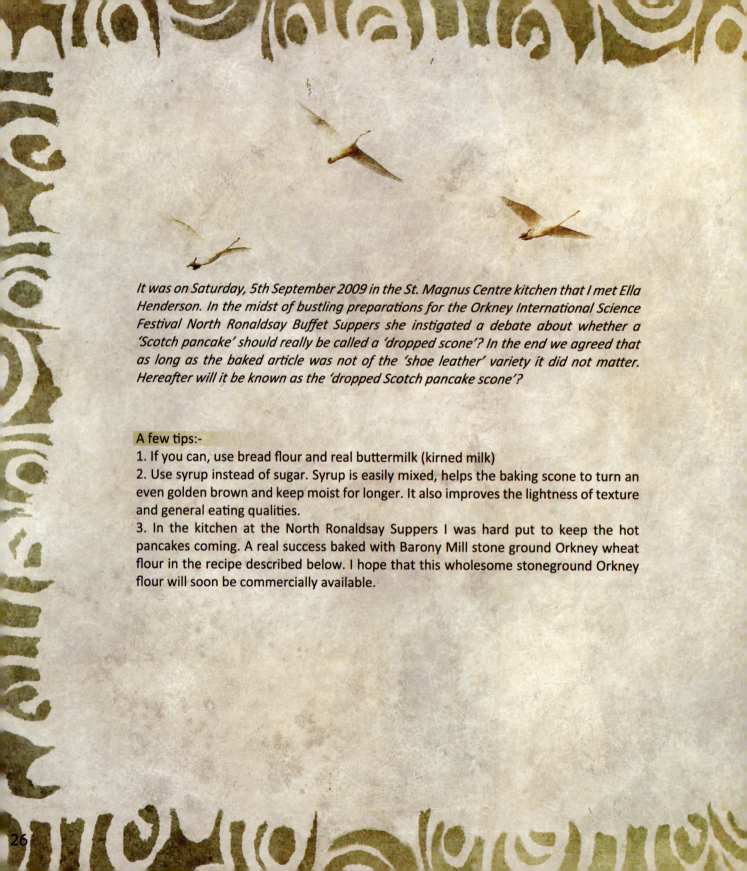

It was on Saturday, 5th September 2009 in the St. Magnus Centre kitchen that I met Ella Henderson. In the midst of bustling preparations for the Orkney International Science Festival North Ronaldsay Buffet Suppers she instigated a debate about whether a 'Scotch pancake' should really be called a 'dropped scone'? In the end we agreed that as long as the baked article was not of the 'shoe leather' variety it did not matter. Hereafter will it be known as the 'dropped Scotch pancake scone'?

A few tips:-

1. If you can, use bread flour and real buttermilk (kirned milk)

2. Use syrup instead of sugar. Syrup is easily mixed, helps the baking scone to turn an even golden brown and keep moist for longer. It also improves the lightness of texture and general eating qualities.

3. In the kitchen at the North Ronaldsay Suppers I was hard put to keep the hot pancakes coming. A real success baked with Barony Mill stone ground Orkney wheat flour in the recipe described below. I hope that this wholesome stoneground Orkney flour will soon be commercially available.

DROPPED SCOTCH PANCAKE SCONES

Makes 18 pancakes
Takes 15 minutes to mix and bake
Bake on a girdle or thick bottomed frying pan

You will need:-
115g (4ozs) Sifted strong white bread flour or a mix 50% white bread flour with 50% Barony Mill stone ground Orkney wheat flour sifted together or sifted plain flour.
1 dessert spoon golden syrup
150mls (0.25pt) approx milk
2 teaspoons baking powder
1 large fresh farm egg

To make:-
1. Heat a girdle, thick bottomed frying pan or hot plate to medium heat.
2. Sift the flour into a bowl, drop in the egg and syrup and gradually add the milk beating well with a balloon whisk (if you have one) or wooden spoon to make a light batter the consistency of thick double cream. Beat in the baking powder last of all.
3. Sprinkle some flour onto the heated cooking surface, if it turns golden brown it is ready to bake. Burnt and it is too hot. When the temperature is correct, shake off the flour and rub with a little cooking oil.
4. Drop table spoons of the batter in rounds onto the hot surface to bake until bubbles appear and begin to pop on the surface.
5. Flip over using a fish slice or palette knife to bake on the other side.
6. Tap the top lightly with the blade of the knife at each flip. This will force out any trapped air to help the turned side bake smoothly.
7. Cool wrapped in a clean tea towel on a wire rack and serve while warm with plenty butter and home made rhubarb and ginger jam.

Cook's tip:-
1. Mix in grated fresh apple with a level teaspoon of cinnamon and bake as above. Serve warm just of the girdle, topped with vanilla ice cream as a dessert.
2. To bake large flat pancakes drop a spoon of batter onto the hot girdle and immediately use the back of the spoon to spread out thinly. The batter will bake quickly, be ready to flip over with the blade of a palette knife. Keep warm in a clean tea towel on a wire tray. Best eaten warm, spread with jam or syrup, roll, bite, enjoy. Watch for the drips!

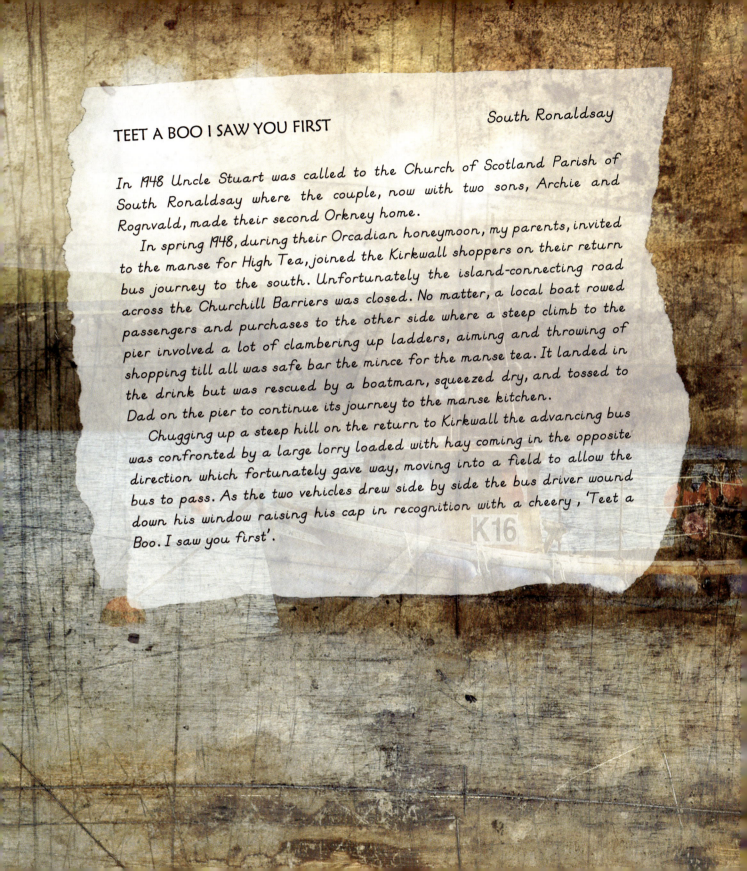

TEET A BOO I SAW YOU FIRST

In 1948 Uncle Stuart was called to the Church of Scotland Parish of South Ronaldsay where the couple, now with two sons, Archie and Rognvald, made their second Orkney home.

In spring 1948, during their Orcadian honeymoon, my parents, invited to the manse for High Tea, joined the Kirkwall shoppers on their return bus journey to the south. Unfortunately the island-connecting road across the Churchill Barriers was closed. No matter, a local boat rowed passengers and purchases to the other side where a steep climb to the pier involved a lot of clambering up ladders, aiming and throwing of shopping till all was safe bar the mince for the manse tea. It landed in the drink but was rescued by a boatman, squeezed dry, and tossed to Dad on the pier to continue its journey to the manse kitchen.

Chugging up a steep hill on the return to Kirkwall the advancing bus was confronted by a large lorry loaded with hay coming in the opposite direction which fortunately gave way, moving into a field to allow the bus to pass. As the two vehicles drew side by side the bus driver wound down his window raising his cap in recognition with a cheery, 'Teet a Boo. I saw you first'.

CHEESY DARTS

This delicious dart has hit many a taste bud bull's eye.

Serves 6 to 8 people
Takes 45 minutes to prepare and cook
Oven bake at 200C, 400F, Gas 6 on the middle shelf.

For short crust you will need:-
225g (8ozs) plain flour
115g (4ozs) margarine
0.25 teaspoon sea salt
Cold water to mix

For filling:-
140g (5ozs) grated Orkney cheddar cheese
30g (1oz) melted butter
2 eggs beaten
Sea salt
Ground black pepper
Pinch of chilli or cayenne pepper

To make:-
1. Turn on the oven to heat and oil a baking tray.
2. Make the pastry. Sift the flour and salt into a bowl, add the margarine and rub in till the mixture is like fine breadcrumbs. Mix to a stiff clean dough with cold water. Set aside to rest.
3. Prepare the filling by mixing the cheese with seasoning, melted butter and beaten egg, reserving some egg to glaze the top of the pastry.
4. Divide the pastry into two, roll one half to fit and line the baking tray. Spread the filling over evenly leaving a small margin round the sides. Roll the rest of the pastry to cover. Press along the sides gently with the tips of your fingers.
5. Brush with the beaten egg and bake fifteen minutes in the middle of the oven till golden.
6. Cool a little, cut into squares and serve hot.

Cook's Tip:-
Use puff pastry instead of short crust.
Experiment with different hard cheeses in the filling

SOUTH RONALDSAY MANSE CHRISTMAS CAKE

Makes 1 x 23cm (9") square, or 25cm (10") round cake
Takes 1 hour to prepare and 11/2hours to bake slowly
Oven bake at 160C, 325F, Gas 3 on the middle shelf

You will need:-

350g (12ozs) Self Raising Flour or plain flour with 2 level teaspoons baking powder added

225g (8ozs) margarine

225g (8ozs) soft brown sugar

Fruit:-

110g (4ozs) sultanas

110g (4ozs) chopped dried apricots (use ready to eat if you can)

110g (4ozs) chopped cherries or try using cranberries instead

175g (6ozs) raisins

2 teaspoons mixed spice

4 large eggs – beaten

Split almonds to decorate

Medium dry sherry (amontillado) to soak

To make:-

1. Line the cake tin. Turn on the oven to heat.
2. Cream the margarine and sugar together till light and fluffy.
3. Sift the dry ingredients together and beat the eggs.
4. Gradually add the eggs to the margarine and sugar mix beating vigorously each time and adding a small amount of sifted flour with each addition to help prevent the mix from curdling.
5. Fold in the rest of the flour stirring gently till all is combined.
6. Stir in the fruit and then put into a lined tin. To prevent the cake rising to a peak in the centre here is a baker's tip. Fill a jug with warm water, dip in your clean hand and using the palm, pat the surface of the uncooked batter to smooth especially in the middle of the tin.
7. Decorate with split almonds.
8. Bake slowly in the middle of the oven for one hour then reduce the heat to 150C, 300F, Gas 2 and bake for a further thirty minutes till firm and the point of a skewer inserted in the middle of the cake comes out cleanly.
9. Cool in the tin, pierce carefully avoiding the almonds and pour over a little sherry to soak while the cake is still warm.
10. Remove from the tin and wrap in greaseproof paper, then a layer of foil and store in an airtight tin to mature for a week before cutting.

Aunt Eileen reckoned that sherry made the best cake, a generous glass for the cook and the rest to pour over the warm cake as it cooled from the long slow baking in the ancient manse range.

SHAPINSAY FERRY DARE

Honeymooners on Orkney, and keen to explore, my father and mother managed to hop aboard the Iona on its delivery day sail to Shapinsay. The Iona was primarily built to carry freight so my parents ended up in the wheel house where spirit flasks and camaraderie abounded.

High tide arrival on Shapinsay allowed an easy disembark with the promise of a few hours to wander while loading and unloading took place. The pair found their way to Balfour Castle where they could wander through grounds left more or less untended during the war years, past rhubarb tall as trees, through overgrown shrubbery and deserted greenhouses, eventually to find an old iron bench at the side of tennis courts where they sat down together.

Tempted by the picnic lunch supplied by the Kirkwall Hotel the honeymooners decided to eat in peace and quiet. Hardly were they mid-sandwich when a piercing, banshee wail brought an abrupt end to the picnic. Full of fright, ready for flight and about to abandon their lunch, they were mightily relieved when all was revealed as two beautiful peacocks appeared from the shrubbery.

Returning to the ferry a few hours later, low tide necessitated a steep climb down a long narrow ladder onto the deck of the waiting Iona. Dressed to impress in tweed suit and hat my mother was very à la mode. She looked down warily at the crewmen at the bottom of the ladder. 'We dare you,' they said.

So, hitching up her skirt, she did!

STIR FRIED RHUBARB RELISH

With Orcadian blood flowing in my veins how could I not love anything rhubarby? Most especially this Christopher Trotter emergency measure to accompany Roast Holmy Lamb.

You will need:-
Fresh rhubarb finely chopped
Fresh root ginger, peeled
Sugar
Balsamic vinegar
Fresh chilli finely chopped (optional)

To make:-
1. Take a wok or thick bottomed frying pan and heat a little vegetable oil.
2. Throw in finely chopped rhubarb fresh from the garden, grate in a little root ginger and keep stirring like mad to soften.
3. Add a dash of balsamic vinegar and a sprinkle of sugar. Turn down the heat and slap on the lid to steam till tender.
4. Taste and season if needed adding a little chopped fresh chilli for an extra 'kick'. Serve with roast lamb or pork.

GREAT AUNT MOLLY'S RICH TEA RHUBARB

Great Aunt Molly was one of the first lady dispensing chemists in Scotland. She was a tall, austere figure with definite ideas about diet and eating, with particular fondness for rhubarb's health giving goodness. She introduced my sisters and me to the delights of her pudding at an early age. It remains a favourite.

Serves 6 people
Takes 45 minutes to prepare and cook.
Allow 1 hour to cool before serving.
Cook on the hob.

You will need:-
450g freshly picked cleaned and chopped rhubarb
2 tablespoons golden syrup
1 packet rich tea biscuits
Water

To make:-

1. Put the rhubarb into a deep pan and spoon the syrup over. Add a little cold water and turn on the heat at medium till bubbling.
2. Stir together then reduce the heat, cover the pan and simmer till tender. The time will depend on the rhubarb. Newly sprouted young tender shoots cook in 1 to 2 minutes, older tougher stems will take longer.
3. Aunt Molly discovered that syrup works to counteract the acidic back taste of rhubarb without being overly sweet.
4. Cool the rhubarb. Serve in individual dishes with tea biscuits to crumble on top.
5. Every Rhubarb Eater has a preference; some like a crisp Rich Tea Topping while others prefer to stir in and await smoother texture, recommended by Great Aunt Molly.

Cook's tip:-

Keep a jar for broken rich tea biscuits, Aunt Molly's accompaniment to rhubarb

RHUBARB AND TAPIOCA

Another childhood favourite.

Serves 4 people
Takes 10 minutes to prepare and
1 hour to bake
Oven Bake at 180C, 350F, Gas 4

You will need:-
450g (1lb) rhubarb washed and chopped
2 level tablespoons tapioca
75g (3ozs) sugar

To make:-

1. Turn on the oven to heat at 180C, 350F, Gas 4 arranging the shelves so that the dish of rhubarb can bake in the middle of the oven.
2. Put the rhubarb into a deep oven proof dish and then sprinkle with the tapioca and sugar.
3. Cover with cold water to fill two thirds of the dish and stir together.
4. Put the dish onto a baking tray to catch drips and bake in the middle of the oven for one hour till set.
5. Serve hot with custard or cold on its own or with cream or yoghurt.

GOING FOR A SPONG

'There are almost as many ways of making marmalade as there are varieties of jam', wrote Orkney's F. Marian McNeill. 'It is an excellent last mouthful at breakfast'.

Perhaps she helped her mother in the Holm manse kitchen with the annual marmalade marathon; bright Seville oranges, golden yellow lemons - scrubbing, de-pipping, pithing, chopping, mincing, boiling, skimming, and potting – bursting with summer sunshine from the stove in dark winter days. No more than twenty marmalade making winters later, in a manse down the road the new minister, Uncle Stuart, and family arrived armed with a technological marmalade manufacturing breakthrough – the 'Spong'! What on earth was this?

My Aunt Eileen bought her Spong, the latest labour saving gadget of its time, at the ironmonger's in Stromness. A forerunner of the food processor, it had a selection of metal cutting cylinders which the aspiring cook could insert into the cavernous depths of its funnel to achieve grating, mincing, chopping or shredding.

This small but amazingly weighty, versatile, hand operated food preparation device required to be clamped to the side of the table to facilitate its use. It was designed for the good old fashioned scrubbed wooden table that was lost with the invention of slippery formica, so steadying its operation involved an ingenious series of screws and precisely chopped pieces of cardboard to ensure it did not budge.

Cranking with one hand and arm while the other held a wooden mallet to press down the ingredient required quite a degree of fortitude when it came to orange peel. Perhaps that is why one of the manse cook book recipes was referred to as General Oldfield's Marmalade. He recommended chopping with a knife and fork!

MANSE MARMALADE

The amount of marmalade yielded by each batch will depend on the fruit used and the simmering time required to achieve a set.

You will need:-
1kg (2.2 lbs) bitter oranges
3 large lemons or 4 small, whatever are available. Choose un-waxed with unblemished skins, sweet oranges, mandarins or satsumas. A ripe juicy pink grapefruit is a good substitute.
Granulated sugar
Glass jars with screw tops or jam pot covers.

To make:-
1. Wash and scrub the fruit, cut into halves, squeeze the juice into a bowl keeping the skins and seeds.
2. Take all the pulp out of the skins and tie along with the seeds into a muslin bag. Use a long piece of string to tie the bag so that it can be attached to the handle of the jam pan. This keeps it out of the way when stirring and prevents it breaking open.
3. Pass the skins through the Spong (set to 'mince') or shred into the jam pan. Alternatively process through a mincing machine or food processor. If all else fails cut by hand!
4. Put the muslin bag into the pan with the minced skins and tie to the handle of the pan. Cover with 3 litres (5pts) water. Stand overnight.
5. The following day simmer slowly for two hours or until the skins are tender. Allow to cool.
6. Remove the muslin bag, squeezing out as much juice as possible because this is an important source of pectin which will help the marmalade to set.
7. Strain the juice into a large bowl and measure back into the pan along with the skins. Add 450g sugar to 600mls (1lb to 1pint) of juice and stir in well, dissolving over a slow heat. Make sure that all the sugar is dissolved before the marmalade comes to the boil. Turn down the heat to simmer for twenty to thirty minutes. Leave the spoon in the pan to prevent the marmalade boiling over and stir frequently to prevent sticking and burning on the bottom of the pan.
8. Test on a saucer for set by dropping a little of the marmalade onto the surface. Leave it for a few minutes and then push the blob with the tip of a clean finger. If it wrinkles the marmalade is simmered enough to set.
9. Cool a little and pour into heated jars. Secure screw top lids while hot or leave to set then cover. Label and store in a cold dark place.

Cook's tip:-
Whisky enhances the flavour of orange marmalade. The secret is to add and stir just before potting. If the marmalade is too hot all the volatile goodness will evaporate in wonderful aromas but little else.

SPEEDY SPONGLESS MARMALADE

No time or, more importantly, no Spong? Try this versatile quickie, easy to adapt to your own taste by adding the citrus fruits of your choice.

You will need:-
1 tin ready prepared marmalade fruit pulp
1 x 3kg bag white granulated sugar
1 large ripe grapefruit, ruby or pink are best or 2 large sweet oranges
1 large lemon

To make:-
1. Wash, chop and de-seed the fresh fruit, cover with cold water, bring to the boil and simmer for ten to fifteen minutes till soft.
2. Process in a food processor or liquidiser along with the ready prepared pulp, rinsing out the tin with cold water to retain all the juices.
3. Put into a suitable jam or deep, thick-bottomed pan with the sugar on a medium heat, stirring all the time till the sugar dissolves.
4. Simmer, stirring occasionally till the marmalade darkens, thickens and when tested on a saucer gives a soft set. Because the marmalade has high fruit content it does not have a firm set.
5. Cool a little in the pan before pouring into jars. Seal with screw on lids while hot or cool and cover. Remember to label the jars. Alternatively the marmalade can be frozen in plastic conatiners.
6. This lower sugar, high fruit marmalade will not keep as long as the traditional high sugar variety therefore it is better kept in the fridge or frozen in plastic containers. Once opened keep in the fridge and use within fourteen days.

Cook's tips:-
Aunt Eileen took F. Marian McNeill's tip and served marmalade with roast pork.
Try stirring in a little balsamic vinegar, a pinch of chilli flakes and fresh chopped ginger to make a tangy orange sauce for roast duck or goose.
Create a hot orange dessert sauce by heating marmalade in a pan, stir in a generous slosh of Cointreau and immediately pour over cold, rich, vanilla ice cream. Serve with fresh orange segments on the side.

CONTRABAND

Known to everyone as the Aunts, Teen and her sister Jess were extremely successful hotel owners.

In 1936 the pair, by then in their sixties, sold the Pentland Hotel in Thurso and retired to live a life of ease in Auld Reekie. Edinburgh could not contain them for long, for after three weeks they became bored. When they discovered that the Standing Stones Hotel at Stenness, close to the ancient Ring of Brodgar, was for sale they flew up on one of the first passenger flights with famous Aviator Captain Ted Fresson and bought the hotel on the spot.

At the beginning of World War II the Aunts were pleased to learn that their newly refurbished acquisition was to be commandeered as Head Quarters of Naval Air Services, providing a hospitality stopover for high ranking service men and their advisors.

I wonder if that is why, despite having no liquor licence, the hotel was known for having the best stocked bar north of Inverness, mostly stored in a downstairs toilet. As a precaution each table in the restaurant was decked with a large vase of flowers which, at any hint of trouble from the law, concealed the offending bottles 'Admirably'.

ORKNEY DARK ISLAND BEEF

During the World Wars food was rationed throughout the United Kingdom. This was a bit of a conundrum for Orcadians because a plentiful supply of local fish, game and beef, could not be ignored. As my Grandmother said, 'use what you've got and you will never want'.

Serves 4 people an all in one oven meal
Takes 3 hours to prepare and cook
Oven cook at 325F, 170C, Gas 3 on the middle shelf

You will need:-

4 trimmed Orkney rib eye or rump steaks – weighing about 150g (5.5oz) to 175g (6ozs) each
3 onions peeled and thinly sliced
225g (6ozs) button mushrooms, cleaned and halved
Sea salt

Marinade

1 tablespoon rape seed or sunflower oil
Freshly ground black pepper
1 clove fresh garlic – peeled and crushed
2 bay leaves
2 teaspoons soft brown or demerara sugar
1 Bottle Orkney Dark Island Beer or similar rich dark ale

To make:-

1. Lay the trimmed steak into a shallow dish. Mix the marinate with 0.25 pint of the beer and pour over. Cover and leave at least two hours or overnight in the fridge.
2. Turn on the oven to heat and arrange the oven shelves to accommodate the meal.
3. Put the steak and marinade into a deep casserole dish, add the onion, mushrooms, and remaining beer. Cover with a tight fitting lid.
4. Put the casserole into a roasting tin and into the oven to cook for two hours.
5. Remove from the oven and stir well, seasoning to taste with sea salt and ground black pepper.
6. Keep warm in the oven while you serve the vegetables – suggestions below.

Cook's tips:-

1. Vegetables: Chop carrot, turnip and onion, place in an oven proof dish, season and pour in a little boiling water. Cover and put on a baking tray. Bake in the oven below the casserole for the last hour, adding a few garden peas for the last ten minutes of cooking time. Drain and serve with the beef.
2. Tatties: Scrub some baking potatoes, prick all over, then slot onto the oven shelves to bake beside the beef for 1.5 hours.

POOR MAN'S STROGANOFF

Another saying was 'Don't put it down, put it away.' A voice which, when I hear it echo from the past, helps to keep the kitchen tidy as I cook. Pity I don't hear it very often!

Serves 6 people
Takes 2.5 hours to prepare and cook
Cook on the hob

You will need:-
675g (1.5lbs) Orkney rump or frying steak, sliced and cut into thin strips
2 large onions, peeled and sliced
450g (1lb) mushrooms, cleaned and sliced
300mls (0.5 pint) dry cider
1 clove garlic, crushed (optional)
300mls (0.5 pint) cream
Nutmeg if you have some
60g (2ozs) butter or 2 tablespoons (30mls) of vegetable oil
Sea salt
Freshly ground black pepper.
Noodles or rice to serve

To make:-
1. Heat half the butter or oil in a deep thick bottomed stew pan then cook the onions and garlic (if used) slowly, stirring till tender and transparent. Remove from the pan, keep warm.
2. Heat the remaining butter or oil and add the meat, stirring over a high heat to brown and seal.
3. Stir in the onions and cider, reduce heat to a slow simmer, cover and cook one hour. Stir occasionally to prevent sticking.
4. Add the sliced mushrooms and cook for a further twenty minutes.
5. Stir in the cream and season to taste with a grating of nutmeg, freshly ground black pepper and a little sea salt. Do not boil.
6. Serve with boiled noodles or rice.

Cook's tip:-
Dry white wine (or similar contraband) can be substituted for the cider.
Chopped fresh parsley scattered over the Stroganoff adds a professional finishing touch.
Use turkey breast or lean pork instead of beef.

THE ORKNEY CLUB

At The Orkney Club time stands still. A heavy oak door opens into a room of wood panelled grandeur where a roaring fire crackles in the grate, warming black leather upholstered chairs of great comfort and size. From these chairs many wise heads have held court or held their peace and, most especially, in times of war the future of our country.

It is a sobering thought that the unobtrusive façade of this harbourside building conceals a living monument to a vital part of war time history. At the top of a polished wooden stair lies the original snooker room where an imposing plaque, endowed by the New Zealand Government in 1919, watches over proceedings. Many of the signatures are barely legible. However, Club member James Watson found a note in the Orkney Archives which gives us a clue to some of the famous names.

'A message cabled from these memory filled rooms on 24th March, 1909 to Sir Joseph Ward, Prime Minister of New Zealand, was signed by members of the House of Commons including: H. H. Asquith (British Liberal Prime Minister, 1908 – 1916). Balfour, Chamberlain, Stanley Baldwin (served three terms as Prime Minister of the United Kingdom). Sir Edward Beauchamp, 1st Baronet (Liberal Party politician who was also chairman of Lloyd's of London from 1905 – 1913). Wedgwood Benn (his mother was a relation of Josiah Wedgwood), Winston Churchill, Henry John Stedman Cotton (Chief Commissioner of Assam), Rupert Guinness, William Peel and Henry Vivian along with many others.'

For many years a comments book and honesty box lay in the corner. Recently the book has been removed to a safe place because it contains comments written by many of history's great men.

The original request funnel to the ground floor catering facilities is in use to this day. Just imagine that this same mouth piece was used by men who in one breath changed the course of history and with another ordered sandwiches, hot pies, and the odd dram. Cigar smoke is a thing of the past, but the atmosphere lingers.

I can picture members of the club relaxing by the crackling fire with a cup of tea or something stronger and a generous hunk of this hearty cake while they 'deliberated, cogitated and ruminated on matters at home and abroad'.

PORTER PLUM CAKE

Makes a cake to fill a tin approximately 18cms (7 inches)
round or 15cms (6inches) square.
Takes 30 minutes to prepare and 1.5 hours to bake.
Oven Bake at 160C, 325F, Gas 3 on the middle shelf

You will need:-
450g (1lb) plain flour
225g (8 ozs) margarine or a mixture of half margarine and half butter
225 g (8ozs) light soft brown sugar or demerara sugar
175 g (6 ozs) raisins
175 g 6ozs) currants
110 g (4ozs) sultanas
110 g (4ozs) mixed peel
3 large eggs
1 teaspoon bicarbonate of soda
1 level teaspoon ground cinnamon
1 level teaspoon ground nutmeg
300 mls (0.5 pint) brisk stout, traditional Orkney beers fit the bill perfectly.

To make:-
1. Prepare the cake tin (see below). Turn on the oven to heat at 160C, 325F, Gas 3.
2. Sift the flour, bicarbonate of soda and spices into a bowl. Add the margarine (and butter if used) cut into small pieces.
3. Using the tips of your fingers to rub the fat into the flour till it resembles fine breadcrumbs.
4. Stir in the sugar and fruit.
5. Mix in the beaten eggs and stout to make a soft batter, then pour into the prepared tin.
6. Bake in the middle of the preheated oven for 1 hour, then reduce the heat to 150C, 300F, Gas 2 for a further thirty minutes or until the cake is risen, firm to touch and the point of a skewer comes out cleanly when inserted into the centre.
7. Cool in the tin on a wire rack. Wrap in greaseproof paper then a layer of foil. Store in an airtight tin in a cool place and wait at least three days before cutting.

Cook's tip:-
For those who don't like mixed peel add chopped apricots or dried cranberries.
A tablespoon of dark chunky marmalade is a good substitute for mixed peel.

TO LINE A CAKE TIN

It is worth taking time to line a cake tin the old fashioned way. The lining protects the cake while it bakes, holds it in good shape, and forms a non-stick, easy to remove jacket which keeps all the moistness trapped in the cake. Best of all the tin is a breeze to clean.

You will need:-
Vegetable oil, pastry brush, ruler or tape measure, greaseproof paper, string, pencil and sharp scissors.

How to:-
1. Lay the tin flat onto the paper and draw round the base, cut out the circle. Repeat.
2. Measure the depth of the tin and multiply by 2.5. Roll out the greaseproof paper flat and measure a strip to that depth from the edge of the paper. To judge the length of the strip the easy way is to stretch string round the outside of the tin, measure and add 4 cms (2inches).
3. Measure the length and cut the strip. Fold in half along its length to give a double thickness of paper. This is the lining for the inside of the tin.
4. Make another fold about 2 cm (1 inch) from the folded edge of the strip. Use the scissors to make small diagonal cuts, about 1cm (0.25 inch) apart, across this smaller fold along the length of the strip.
5. Use the pastry brush to oil the inside of the baking tin.
6. Lay the first circle into the base and brush with oil.
7. Making sure that the slashed fold sits round the base of the tin, ease the long strip round the inside of the tin, smoothing the paper onto the oiled surface and flattening the snipped edges at right angles onto the base.
8. Paint with oil. Place the final disc onto the base of the tin to cover all the jagged edges and paint with oil.
9. It is important to make sure that all the jagged edges are covered and that the paper is not wrinkled. This is what makes sure that the cake is 'in good shape'.
10. With practice this becomes easy and a useful skill, for, the same applies to all shapes of cake tin. A well lined tin is especially important when making large rich cakes which require long slow baking because the lining acts as a protection to prevent them drying out, retaining a good moist texture and flavour.

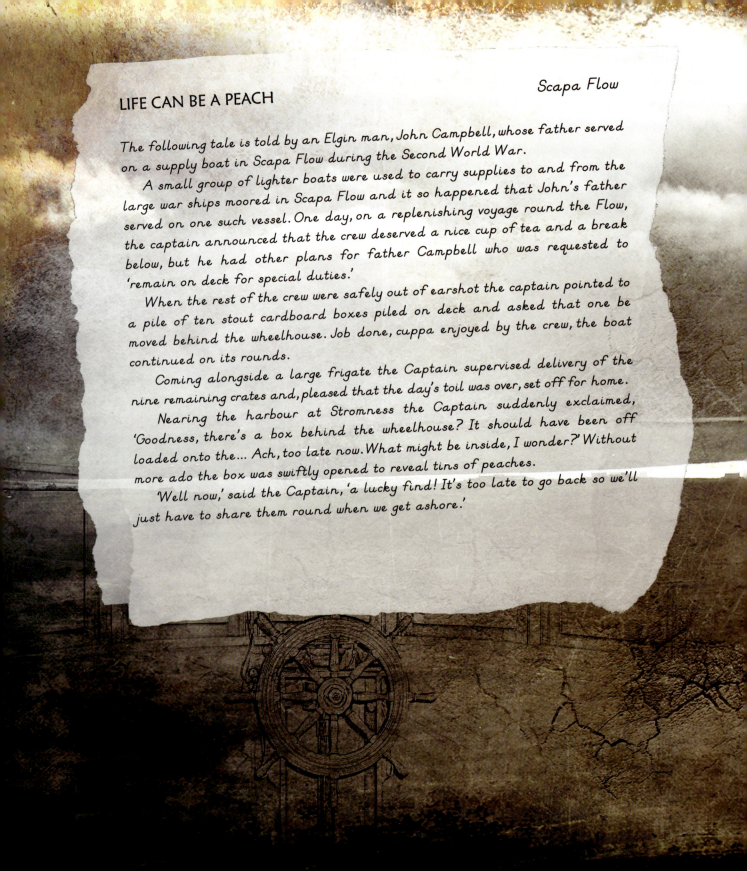

LIFE CAN BE A PEACH

Scapa Flow

The following tale is told by an Elgin man, John Campbell, whose father served on a supply boat in Scapa Flow during the Second World War.

A small group of lighter boats were used to carry supplies to and from the large war ships moored in Scapa Flow and it so happened that John's father served on one such vessel. One day, on a replenishing voyage round the Flow, the captain announced that the crew deserved a nice cup of tea and a break below, but he had other plans for father Campbell who was requested to 'remain on deck for special duties.'

When the rest of the crew were safely out of earshot the captain pointed to a pile of ten stout cardboard boxes piled on deck and asked that one be moved behind the wheelhouse. Job done, cuppa enjoyed by the crew, the boat continued on its rounds.

Coming alongside a large frigate the Captain supervised delivery of the nine remaining crates and, pleased that the day's toil was over, set off for home.

Nearing the harbour at Stromness the Captain suddenly exclaimed, 'Goodness, there's a box behind the wheelhouse? It should have been off loaded onto the... Ach, too late now. What might be inside, I wonder?' Without more ado the box was swiftly opened to reveal tins of peaches.

'Well now,' said the Captain, 'a lucky find! It's too late to go back so we'll just have to share them round when we get ashore.'

PEACH SPONGE PUDDING

It is more than likely that those self-same peaches would have borne the famous brand name of SPC. It is however, a little known fact that the SPC peach growing estate was so vast that they had their own Post Office address at Mataffan. Life-long family friends whose elderly aunt was governess to, and lived all her adult life with, the SPC family once sent a case as a gift during a visit to South Africa and that is how we found out.

Makes a nice pudding for 4
Takes 1 hour to make
Oven 180C, 350F, Gas 4 on the middle shelf

You will need:-
1 medium size tin of sliced peaches
85g (3ozs) margarine
85g (3ozs) plain flour
2 teaspoons baking powder
85g (3ozs) caster sugar
2 eggs - separated
1 level teaspoon ground cinnamon (optional)

To make:-
1. Turn on the oven to heat. Oil the inside of an ovenproof dish.
2. Sift the flour, baking powder and cinnamon together.
3. Drain the peaches, reserve the juice and put the drained peaches into the bottom of the prepared dish.
4. Cream the margarine and sugar together till soft and fluffy then beat in the egg yolks.
5. Gently fold in the sifted flour mixture along with the saved juice.
6. Beat the egg whites till stiff and fold into the sponge mixture.
7. Pour over the peaches and bake in the middle of the oven for about forty minutes till golden on top and firm to the touch.
8. Remove from the oven and serve at once with plenty cold cream or ice cream.

GRILLED GAMMON WITH PEACHES

Serves 2 people
Takes 30 minutes to make
Grill or oven

You will need:-
2 gammon steaks, trimmed
1 small tin of peaches, drained

Marinade:-
1 tablespoon sunflower or vegetable oil
1 tablespoon peach juice
1 level teaspoon ground ginger
Generous pinch of chilli flakes
Generous pinch of ground cinnamon
2 teaspoons runny honey

To make:-
1.Line the grill pan with aluminium foil to prevent the juices burning causing a difficult wash up operation. Turn on the grill at medium to high.
2.Make a mix of 1 tablespoon vegetable or sunflower oil with one level teaspoon ground ginger, generous pinch of chilli flakes, two teaspoons runny honey and a little ground cinnamon.
3.Using a sharp knife slash the edges of the gammon steaks to prevent them curling up as they grill. Spread a third of the marinade over one side of the gammon steaks and put onto the lined grill pan to cook.
4.Grill for three to four minutes then turn and spread the other side. Reserving the last third of the mixture. Grill a further two minutes. Mix the remains of the marinade with the peaches and use to top the gammon steaks.
5.Grill a further three to four minutes to heat through.
6.Serve hot. Any left can be chopped and added to rice or pasta salad.
7.Can be baked 'all in one' in the oven set at 190C, 375F, Gas No 5.

Cook's Tip:-
The marinade makes great barbecued chicken legs or sticky grilled sausages.

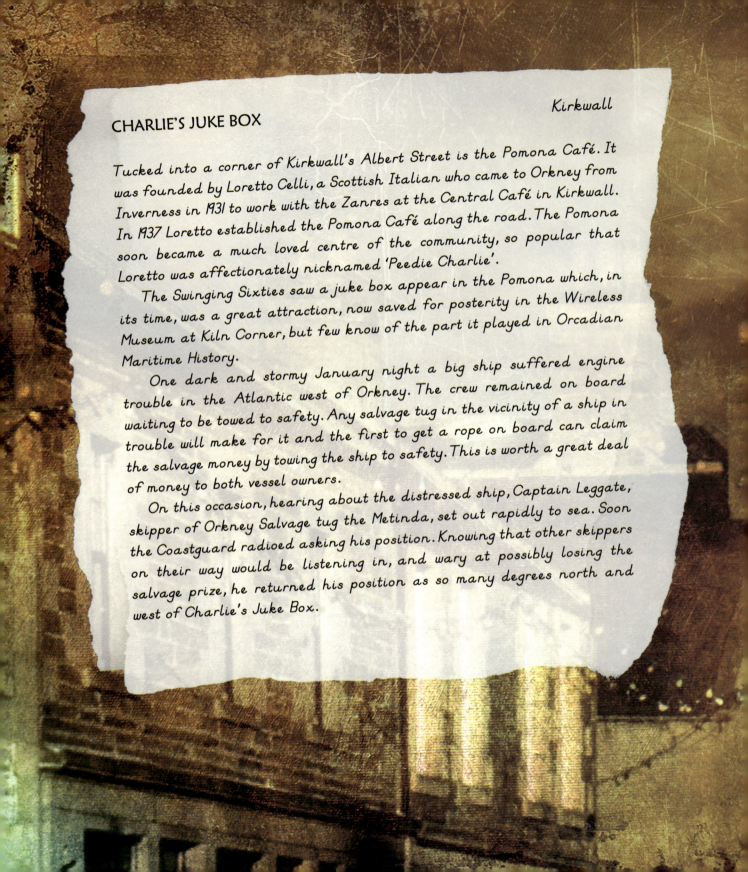

CHARLIE'S JUKE BOX

Tucked into a corner of Kirkwall's Albert Street is the Pomona Café. It was founded by Loretto Celli, a Scottish Italian who came to Orkney from Inverness in 1931 to work with the Zanres at the Central Café in Kirkwall. In 1937 Loretto established the Pomona Café along the road. The Pomona soon became a much loved centre of the community, so popular that Loretto was affectionately nicknamed 'Peedie Charlie'.

The Swinging Sixties saw a juke box appear in the Pomona which, in its time, was a great attraction, now saved for posterity in the Wireless Museum at Kiln Corner, but few know of the part it played in Orcadian Maritime History.

One dark and stormy January night a big ship suffered engine trouble in the Atlantic west of Orkney. The crew remained on board waiting to be towed to safety. Any salvage tug in the vicinity of a ship in trouble will make for it and the first to get a rope on board can claim the salvage money by towing the ship to safety. This is worth a great deal of money to both vessel owners.

On this occasion, hearing about the distressed ship, Captain Leggate, skipper of Orkney Salvage tug the Metinda, set out rapidly to sea. Soon the Coastguard radioed asking his position. Knowing that other skippers on their way would be listening in, and wary at possibly losing the salvage prize, he returned his position as so many degrees north and west of Charlie's Juke Box.

OLD MEN OF HOY

Named after the Old Man of Hoy, baked to resemble that famous crag of rock and topped with a blob of runny white icing to represent what sea birds do on rocks apart from nesting.

Makes 6 to 8 cakes
Takes 20 minutes to prepare and 20 minutes to bake
Oven bake at 180C, 350F, Gas 4 on the middle shelf

For cakes you will need:-
115g (4ozs) soft margarine
115g (4ozs) caster sugar
2 eggs
115g (4ozs) self raising flour
1 level teaspoon baking powder
Pinch of salt

For coating:-
4 tablespoons of red jam mixed with 1 tablespoon water
60g (2ozs) desiccated coconut

For topping:-
Glacé icing: mix icing sugar with water or lemon juice till smooth.
8 Glacé cherry halves

To make:-
1. Turn on the oven to heat. Grease eight dariole, or castle, pudding moulds.
2. Cream the margarine and sugar till light and fluffy.
3. Sift the flour, baking powder and salt into a bowl.
4. Gradually beat the eggs into the margarine mixture alternately with a little flour.
5. Fold the remaining sifted flour into the mixture then divide evenly between the moulds. Smooth with the back of a metal spoon dipped in warm water, making a small dip in the centre to prevent the sponge rising to a peak. Put the filled moulds on a baking tray.
6. Bake in the middle of the oven for twenty minutes till risen, golden and firm. Cool in the tins on a wire tray.
7. Remove the cooled cakes from the tins and cut to make a flat base if needed.
8. Heat the jam and water in a pan and boil one minute stirring all the time.
9. Put the coconut onto a sheet of greaseproof paper, brush the sides and narrow top of each cake with jam, roll in the coconut and lay, base down, on a flat plate.
10. Use two teaspoons to drop icing on top, with Number One as a scoop and the back of Number Two to push the icing onto the cake. Place a half glacé cherry in the centre.

EMILY'S CHOCOLATE GATEAU

Definitely not for the calorie conscious.

Makes a round tin 20cm (8inches) in diameter
Takes 1.5 hours to prepare and bake
Oven bake at 160C, 325F, Gas 3 on the middle shelf

You will need:-
280g (10ozs) plain flour sifted with 2
teaspoons baking powder and pinch salt
225g (8ozs) soft margarine
175g (6ozs) soft brown sugar
60g (2ozs) cocoa powder
4 large eggs
Hot water

Filling and coating:-
225g (8ozs) sifted icing sugar
75g (2.5ozs) cocoa powder dissolved
in a little boiling water
115g (4ozs) soft margarine
1 teaspoon vanilla essence
Chocolate vermicelli

To make:-

1. Turn on the oven to heat.
2. Cream the sugar and margarine till light and fluffy. Beat the eggs.
3. Beat the eggs in alternately with a little sifted flour. Fold in the remaining flour.
4. Dissolve the cocoa in hot water to make a smooth, slightly runny paste. Fold into the cake mixture.
5. Put into a lined cake tin, smooth the top with the palm of your hand dipped in warm water, making a small dip in the middle to prevent the cake rising in a peak.
6. Bake thirty minutes then reduce the oven temperature to 160C, 300F, Gas 2 a further twenty to thirty minutes, or till the point of a skewer comes out cleanly. Cool in the tin.
7. While the cake is cooling make the chocolate butter cream icing to fill and coat.
8. Beat the margarine with the icing sugar till light. Mix the cocoa powder with hot water to make a smooth paste, beat into the icing with the vanilla essence.
9. Cut the cooled cake in three layers and sandwich together with icing. Coat the top and sides with icing using a flat bladed knife. Retain enough to pipe on the top.
10. Spoon a pile of chocolate vermicelli onto the middle of a sheet of greaseproof paper. Hold the cake over the greaseproof paper with the base on the flat palm of your left hand and use your right palm to lift and press the chocolate vermicelli lightly onto the sides. The excess will fall onto the paper and can be used again.
11. Put onto a cake board or serving plate, pipe with butter cream round the base and top.

THE BACKROOM BOYS

Around the year 1930 John Gow, an elderly bachelor living in the Albert Hotel, was a Maths teacher at Kirkwall Grammar School. Seeking company he became friendly with Peedie Charlie, owner of the Pomona Café where they would often pass time chatting, seated by the stove in the back room. Sometimes John would go out with another friend to rake cockles at low tide which they would scatter on top of that same stove. In the heat the cockles would open and cook in their own juice and in this way, eating fresh cockles and blethering, there began what grew into the informal club known as The Backroom Boys.

Over the years doctors and teachers, lawyers and bankers, friends fae a' airts would gather to 'discuss things', putting their world to rights over cups of coffee and huge plates of digestive biscuits. The Backroom Boys continued through the War and so popular did the institution become that local art teacher George Scott, fortified by his daily Pomona ice cream cone, created a four feet (1.22m) high by eight feet (2.44m) wide oil painting of club members during the late 1950s. This large painting hung for many years on the wall above the fire in the back room but has been moved upstairs as the back room is used differently now.

In the natural progression of things the Backroom Boys numbers dwindled but the characters are kept alive by George's unique masterpiece signed by the artist himself and dated 14/1/1959.

MUSSEL AND SPOOT BREE

Razor clams (known on Orkney as spoots) are, like cockles, free to anyone who wanders along Orkney's sandy beaches. A Christopher Trotter recipe.

First catch your spoot:-
Tide out. Walking backwards, pluck spoots from the sand as they pop up. Put into a bucket of fresh water.

Ready to cook
Wash the catch thoroughly in fresh running water. Cockles, mussels and spoots,use the shellfish you have or prefer.

Makes enough to serve 4 to 6 people
Takes 45 minutes to prepare, cook and serve
Cook on the hob

You will need:-
450g (1lb) roughly chopped vegetable mixture of carrots, celery, onion. This is called in French mirepoix, which means mixture and is named after the French Duc de Mirepoix a chef of history.
1kg (2.2lbs) mussels (cockles can be cooked this way also)
8 spoots
125mls (4.5ozs) white wine or cider
30g (1oz) butter
1 medium size leek cut length wise then finely sliced
Water
30g (1oz) shredded wild garlic or fresh parsley
150mls (5fl ozs) double cream

To make:-
1.You need two pans, one to cook the shellfish and the other to cook the bree.
2.Place the mirepoix, wine, mussels or cockles and spoots in the first pan. Cover with a tight fitting lid and cook gently till the spoots are open, this should take about five minutes, set aside.
3.In the second pan sweat the leek in the butter over a low heat till soft but not coloured for about ten minutes, stirring occasionally to prevent sticking.
4.While this is cooking remove the mussels from the pan and either remove from their shell or loosen. Put into a warmed serving tureen or bowl.
5.Remove the spoots from their shells, discarding the stomach sack. Slice the spoot flesh into small chunks. Add to the mussels in the bowl.

6. Strain the cooking liquid into the leek mixture when it is cooked and add 300mls (0.5pt) water simmer for three to four minutes, add the cream and parsley or wild garlic and return to the boil.

7. Season to taste at the last minute with a little sea salt, pour over the mussels and spoots and serve in heated dishes with a generous wedge of Orkney bere meal bannock.

A HOME MADE DIGESTIVE BISCUIT

Did you know extensive market research has revealed that if a woman shopping for biscuits is confronted with a huge display she will, in the end, select what is familiar? Nine times out of ten this is a packet of digestives. Furthermore the secret of a good biscuit is an empty plate. Created to honour those 'Digestive Connoisseurs' the Back Room Boys.

Make 30 biscuits 6cm (2.5 inches) in diameter
Takes 45 minutes to make
Oven bake 180C, 350F, Gas 4 above the middle shelf.

You will need:-
115g (4ozs) plain flour
115g (4ozs) fine oatmeal
30g (1oz) soft brown sugar
60g (2ozs) vegetable margarine
1 level teaspoon baking powder
Pinch of salt
Cold water to mix

To make:-
1. Turn on the oven to heat.
2. Put all the ingredients into a mixing bowl and rub the fat into the flour till it resembles fine bread crumbs.
3. Mix to a smooth clean dough, similar to short crust pastry, with a little cold water.
4. Turn onto a floured surface and roll out to 0.25cm (1/8inch) thickness.
5. Cut into rounds, prick twice with a fork and lay onto a lightly oiled or non-stick baking tray. This will release any trapped air from the dough as the biscuit bakes. That is why commercially baked biscuits are often ringed with small holes, they are known as 'tickles'.
6. Bake at 180C, 350F, Gas 4 for 15 minutes or till crisp and golden brown. Check the tray after eight minutes and turn to allow even cooking. Watch carefully as these biscuits can burn easily.
7. Cool a little on the baking tray and then on a wire rack. Store in an airtight tin.

Cooks tip:-
Use medium oatmeal to make a rough crunchy texture.
May all your biscuit plates be empty!

SAMUEL THE CRAB

Several years ago Radio Orkney personality, Howie Firth found himself in the role of judge at the prestigious Pets Competition held during the annual Gala holiday known as 'Stromness Shopping Week'. All was going according to plan until a Committee Official discovered that 'The Most Unusual Pet Category' was completely vacant — no entries at all.

Perhaps no-one had a pet different enough to enter but, taking into consideration the bruised feelings of the Award's generous donor, an announcement was made over the loudspeaker encouraging last minute entries. No takers! A second, more vociferous plea caught the attention of a group of young men who, at that precise moment, were emerging from a nearby hostelry. Fortified by their recent refreshment they gallantly accepted the challenge by producing a large crab.

The crab's 'owner' gave a moving description of his inseparable relationship with 'Samuel', a friendship which had grown steadily since the crustacean had first appeared in one of his lobster pots.

Judge Howie had a decision to make but, with no other unusual pets forthcoming and the press photographer poised to take a shot of the beaming duo, what could he do? Turning a very blind eye to Samuel's inert condition he handed the handsome prize to the competition's sole entry. The owner and his entourage then removed the inactive winner from the scene, retracing their steps to the bar. Prize-winning can be a thirsty business.

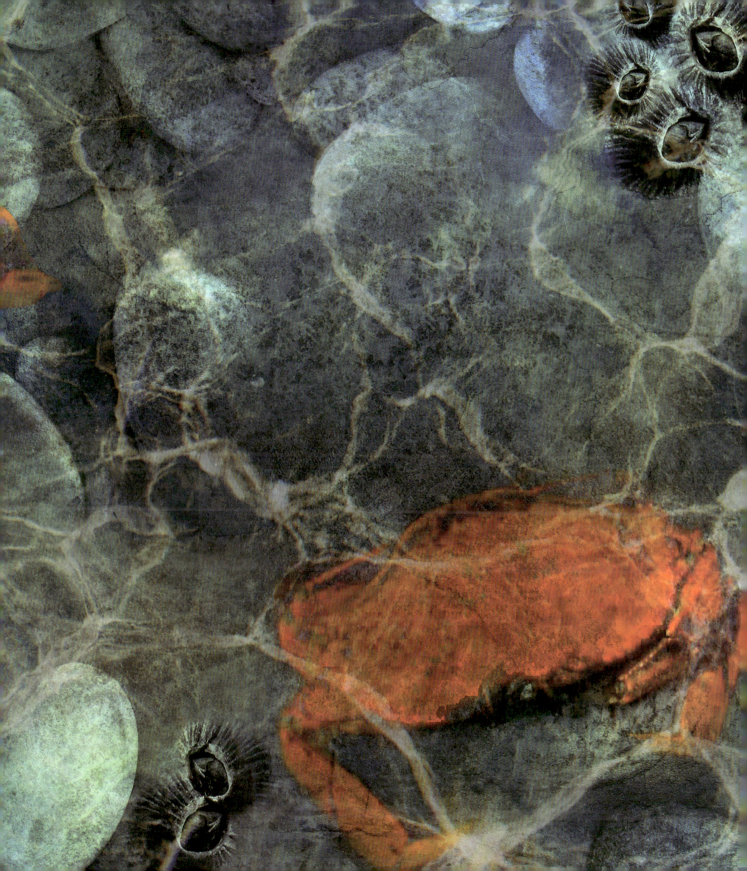

CENTENARY ORKNEY CRAB TATTIE

Well known Orcadian Kathleen Firth celebrated her 100th birthday on June 14th 2009. One of her favourite eats is a baked Orkney tattie, brim full of fresh Orkney white crab meat with a hint of mayonnaise. Is this a key to her longevity?

SMOKED SALMON AND CRAB TIMBALE

Paul Doull's recipe is simple and will impress.

Serves 4
Takes about five minutes to prepare plus
at least 1 hour chilling time.
No cooking required

You will need:-
200g (7oz) pack Orkney smoked salmon slices
1 pot Orkney crab pate or picked white Orkney crab meat, approximately 225g (8ozs)
Garnish:- Rocket leaves, cherry tomatoes, lemon wedges and parsley

To make:-
1. Line four ramekin dishes with slices of smoked salmon leaving enough to trail over the side to form a lid.
2. Fill the cavity with crab and then lift the slices over to cover. Chill for at least one hour before serving.
3. Turn out onto the centre of a flat serving plate with garnish on the side.

Cook's tip:-
A mixture of 50% brown and 50% white crab meat can be used instead.

FISH STOCK

Make in bulk, freeze any surplus in small containers and as ice cubes as a standby.

You will need:-
225g (8ozs) fish trimmings and bones.
1 litre (1.75pts) cold water
1 stalk celery
1 small leek
a few peppercorns
1 bay leaf

To make:-

1. Wash the fish trimmings and put into a pan with the vegetables and cold water.
2. Crab, lobster or similar shells can be added give a rich shellfish flavour if required.
3. Boil, skim, reduce the heat, cover and simmer thirty minutes. Strain and use as needed.

PARTAN BREE

A partan is the local name for the edible crab and bree is the stock or soup in which it is cooked. Christopher Trotter made his version using fresh prepared Orkney crab for convenience. He suggests using brown crab meat in the soup and white as a garnish stirred through at the last minute.

Serves 6 to 8 people
Takes 30 minutes to prepare and cook
Cook on the hob.

You will need:-
200g (7ozs) brown crab meat
100g (3.5ozs) white crab meat
100g (3.5ozs) butter
1 onion peeled and finely chopped
100g (3.5ozs) fine oatmeal. (Barony Mill Orkney Oatmeal F1)
600mls (1pt) hot fish or crab stock
600mls (1pt) milk
Sea Salt
Ground mixed peppercorns or black peppercorns

To finish:-
Double cream and/or malt whisky
Freshly chopped herbs such as parsley, coriander, chervil or wild garlic.

To make:-

1. Stir the onion with the butter in a large soup pan over a low heat till soft, not coloured.
2. Stir in the oatmeal then slowly add the stock stirring till it thickens and forms a light 'porridge'.
3. Use a balloon whisk to lightly whisk in the brown crab meat and milk.
4. Bring slowly to the boil and simmer a few minutes stirring continuously.
5. Season to taste and finish with a little double cream and/or a dram of whisky. Serve in heated bowls scattered with freshly chopped mixed herbs.

Cook's tip:-
A grinding of red, white, green and black peppercorns complements the flavour of fish, shellfish and cured or smoked salmon.

A DAUGHTER OF HOLM

F. Marion McNeill was born on the Orkney Mainland village of Holm, a daughter of the Free Church minister. She became a journalist in Edinburgh and was, in fact, quite a radical for her day and a founder of what is now known as the Scottish National Party. Interested in her country's folk lore and heritage she is best remembered for her books The Scots Kitchen and The Scots Cellar which she researched and wrote with characteristic dry wit. When, in 1933, Alexander MacLehose and Company published the innovative books The Campers Kitchen and The Book of Breakfast she was described by a literary critic in The Daily Telegraph as 'A dangerous woman out to wreck the rights of the subject to be "grumpy" at breakfast.'

In 1984 a friend gave me a copy of The Scots Kitchen and I could not put it down. After devouring that book and Scottish Cookery, written by my former teacher Catherine Brown, I was inspired to write what became Teach the Bairns, a Scottish cookery series for beginners of all ages. That Christmas a review of the book in the Sunday Times gave me the finest accolade I could have wished for as 'F. Marion McNeill made easy.'

F. Marion McNeill was a close friend of Gordon Baxter of Baxters of Speyside. When I worked there as Catering Manager it seems that I may have served her in the Directors' Dining Room. It is an exciting possibility but, sadly, it can never be verified as she died in 1973. After her death Catherine put into words what we both, as individuals as well as part of the wider cooking community feel. 'Our debt to her is infinite.' In fact, her books were, and remain for us, an inspiration.

The writings of F. Marian McNeill reveal little about the food she herself enjoyed. Re-reading my well-worn copy of The Scots Kitchen I came to the conclusion that the only dishes about which she makes personal comment are those she would have eaten at home on Orkney.

RUMBLED FINNAN HADDIE

F.Marian McNeill writes of her enjoyment of windblown fish, these are salted, wind dried overnight, rolled in flour and cooked over a slow fire. 'In Orkney cuithes are prepared in this way. They may be brandered or boiled and eaten with melted butter. ' Windblown fish are indeed delicious but not so widely available, so, I have created this similar dish in its stead. Why rumbled? The fish is stirred or 'rumbled' in the pan to make a smooth texture.

Makes enough for 4 to enjoy
Takes 20 minutes to prepare and cook
Cook on the hob

You will need:-
115g (4ozs) cooked Finnan Haddock or similar fish
45g (1.5ozs) butter softened
1 tablespoon of cream
1 tablespoon chopped fresh parsley (if available)
Freshly ground black pepper
Fresh lemon juice
Sea salt

To make:-
1. Flake the cooked fish and remove all bones.
2. Melt the butter in a saucepan, stir in the flaked fish and cream stirring vigorously to make a smooth paste.
3. Season to taste with plenty ground black pepper and a little lemon juice. You may not require sea salt as smoked fish has already been salted.
4. Stir to heat through and serve hot sprinkled with fresh parsley.

Cook's tip:-
Try making this recipe with the sweet succulent flesh of Orkney Hot Roast Smoked Salmon or an old fashioned Arbroath Smokie.

POSH PORRIDGE

She insists that the only way to serve porridge should be in large soup plates with small bowls of cream, milk or buttermilk at the side. 'The porridge must be very hot and the bowl of cream or milk, in contrast, quite cold.' There is a belief stemming from Druid times that stirring or passing round food must be done clockwise following the sun, known as deiseal. It was thought unlucky to stir in a left-hand direction or widdershins. I wonder if she would have liked like my friend Colin's 'Posh Porridge'. It is always 'rightly' stirred.

Makes 2 servings or one huge plateful
Takes 10 minutes to prepare and cook
Cook on the hob or microwave for three minutes on approx 700w power level

You will need:-
0.5 cup medium oatmeal
1.5 cups water
A small handful of raisins
And/or
A small handful of chopped dates
A small handful of roasted hazelnuts crushed
0.5 teaspoon ground cinnamon
(less rather than more)
0.5 teaspoon powdered ginger
(if you like ginger)
2 teaspoons dark soft brown sugar
0.5 teaspoon salt

To make:-
1. Put the oatmeal and water into a pan and keep stirring till it boils.
2. Reduce the heat and allow the porridge to simmer for about five minutes. Remember to stir occasionally to stop the porridge sticking to the pan.
3. Add the other ingredients of your choice and simmer, stirring for another three or four minutes.
4. Or Microwave cook on approx 700w power level for two minutes, stir in the other ingredients and cook a further two minutes. Stir and serve.
5. Serve hot but remember to taste first.

Cook's tip:-
Make a faster version using flaked porridge oats. Put all the ingredients into a pan and bring to the boil stirring all the time. Simmer stirring for three to four minutes and serve.

TAKING THE BISCUITS

In the early 2000s I was given the opportunity to work with Orkney Herring. The owner, Ken Sutherland, also engaged two other food manufacturing experts with whom I made my first ferry trip to Orkney on the MV Hamnavoe. Affectionately known as Graham and Our Garry this duo are dead ringers for Little and Large both in stature and good humour.

Graham, as well as being a brilliant food scientist, is also an eminent ornithologist who at one time was warden of a bird reserve in the Cairngorm National Park. Our Garry is a typical witty Liverpudlian, a great foil for the giant Graham. Our work was finished more quickly than expected and Graham took us on a twitcher's tour of Mainland Orkney. His enthusiasm quickly transferred to Gary and me. The highlight was sitting in the bird hide at Loch of the Louns watching a giant heron lording it like the Mikado over a family of mandarin ducks.

I was under strict instructions from my parents to return with beremeal biscuits from the local bakery but when we returned to Stromness I found that it was closed. We went our separate ways planning to meet in the evening in the Royal Hotel.

Later, when I passed the bakery en route to the Royal I noticed, lo and behold, the shop had reopened. 'Do you have any beremeal biscuits, please,' I asked the assistant inside.

'Yes, you can have the last two packets,' she said, popping them into a carrier bag. 'It's very strange, but we've had quite a run on them this evening.'

At the hotel I found Our Garry at the bar. Beaming from ear to ear he lifted a bulging carrier bag. 'I noticed that the bakery had reopened,' he said. 'I bought these for your father.'

With that Graham arrived carrying yet another bulging bag with, yes, you've guessed it. BEREMEAL BISCUITS!

WAFFLE BISCUITS

I love baking biscuits and this is the first recipe I was allowed to bake solo. My training involved mastering the waffle fork cross marking technique.

Takes 30 minutes to prepare and bake
Oven bake at 180C, 350F,
Gas 4 above the middle shelf

You will need:-
60g (2ozs) sugar
60g (2ozs) golden syrup
60g (2ozs) white vegetable fat
60g (2ozs) margarine
½ teaspoon bicarbonate of soda
½ teaspoon ground ginger
175g (6ozs) self raising flour

To make:-
1. Turn on the oven to heat. Prepare two baking trays by rubbing them with kitchen towel dipped in a little cooking oil.
2. Sift the flour and ginger together into a bowl
3. Melt the sugar, fat, margarine and syrup in a pan.
4. Beat in the bicarbonate of soda till the mixture fluffs.
5. Beat in the sifted flour to make a smooth paste.
6. Take two teaspoons to spoon the mixture onto the baking trays. Scoop with one and use the back of the other to push onto the tray leaving space between the biscuits to spread as they bake.
7. Dip a fork in hot water and use the back to press each biscuit flat and then across to make a waffle pattern. Dipping in hot water stops sticking to the fork.
8. Bake in the pre-heated oven for fifteen minutes. Check after ten minutes; swap the trays to ensure even browning if needed.
9. Cool on the trays a little then lift with a flat bladed knife onto a wire-cooling tray.
10. Store in an airtight tin when cold. Important as the biscuits will soften if left.

Cook's tip:-
Adding a pinch of chilli powder enhances the flavour of ginger. Don't add too much.

LEMON SHORTIES

The Clarke family lived next door to my childhood home, Mummy Clarke, Auntie Mary and son Donald, a giant over six feet tall. He became a well known athlete at Highland games tossing large cabers and putting even heavier shots. No doubt his mother's home baking had a lot to do with his feats of stamina and strength. These little biscuits were one of her specialities.

Makes 12 little melt in the mouth biscuits
Takes 30 minutes to prepare and bake
Oven bake at 190C, 375F, Gas 5 on the middle shelf

For the biscuits you will need:-
Biscuits
115g (4ozs) margarine
60g (2ozs) margarine
Grated rind of 1 lemon
115g (4ozs) plain flour
1 level teaspoon baking powder

For the icing:-
Icing sugar
Freshly squeezed lemon juice
Chocolate vermicelli

To make:-
1. Turn on the oven to heat and adjust the shelves so that the shorties can bake in the middle of the oven.
2. Cream the margarine and icing sugar till light and fluffy in texture.
3. Beat in the lemon rind and flour.
4. Place in teaspoons on an oiled baking tray leaving space for the biscuits to spread as they bake.
5. Bake in the middle of the oven for fifteen minutes till pale golden. Cool on a wire tray.
6. Make water icing with the fresh lemon juice and use the back of a teaspoon to coat the top of each cooled biscuit.
7. Sprinkle with chocolate vermicelli to decorate.

Cook's tip:-
Replace the lemon with orange to make orange shorties.
Sometimes Mummy Clarke made a mix and match, lemon shorties with orange icing and vice-versa.

FIRE ALARM

A few years ago John Clarke, who founded Orkney the Brand and ran a very successful press liaison programme, invited several members of the Guild of Food Writers on a visit. In those days I was a very junior addition to their numbers and extremely grateful for John's knowledge and guiding hand.

A most eagerly anticipated visit was to the Orkney Fisherman's Society Crab Factory at Stromness. Taking into consideration the strict hygiene preparations required before factory entry is permitted we had probably been on site for an hour being hosed down, hatted, overalled and booted before entry into the inner sanctums. Concentrating on the interesting commentary and not wishing to miss a single moment we were suddenly stopped in our crab reveries by the shrill insistent ringing of the Fire Alarm.

No practice, this was For Real! Ushered in all our finery to the muster point outside we waited patiently, until two Fire Engines came screaming to a halt. The fire fighters ran inside wielding axes and hoses until, after what seemed like an age, the all clear sounded. Sadly for us there was no time left to complete the visit, the crab secrets had to be left in Stromness for another day.

A few years passed and I found myself sitting in the bar of the Pierowall Hotel in Westray where I happened to meet a gentleman in a blue boiler suit and his very young looking apprentice. It transpired that they had arrived from Stromness to work on the new Deep Freeze part of the Westray Crab Factory, also owned by Orkney Fishermen's Society.

During the conversation I was asked if I had ever visited the parent factory. Yes and no, I replied. As I relayed the above tale the young apprentice become extremely red in the face and distinctly uncomfortable until he confessed that the fire alarm had been of his doing. He had tripped over his regulation 'Muckle White Wellies' and fallen onto the button.

ANN'S HADDOCK AND PRAWN FISH PIE

I am a self-confessed Orkney tattie addict. Imagine my delight when I arrived at Rapness to catch the Kirkwall ferry, to be greeted by the waitress from the hotel with a large bag of, yes you've guessed it, Westray tatties to take home. That same waitress, Alison Pottinger, is the wife of the farmer who grows Westray tatties. How good were those spuds? Teamed with Pierowall fish, so fresh it hardly knows it's been caught , a winning partnership as traditional fish and chips or my friend Ann Rendall's fish pie.

Serves 4 people
Takes 1 hour to make and bake
Cook – hob and oven
Can be made in advance and kept in the fridge.

You will need:-
30g (1oz) butter or margarine
30g (1oz) plain flour
300mls (0.5pt) milk
Fresh lemon juice
1 dessertspoon mayonnaise
1 tablespoon freshly chopped parsley
or 1 teaspoon dried if you have no fresh
225g (8ozs) fresh haddock
175g (6ozs) fresh cooked prawns
675 g (1.5lb) Orkney tatties, peeled
Milk and butter to mash
Salt and ground black pepper

To make:-
1. Poach the haddock in the milk till tender. Flake the fish, reserving the milk to make the parsley sauce.
2. Put the potatoes on to cook in boiling salted water and while they are cooking make the sauce.
3. Melt the margarine or butter, stir in the flour and then gradually stir in the reserved milk stirring all the time till the sauce thickens and boils.
4. Reduce the heat and beat in the mayonnaise, a little fresh lemon juice, sea salt and freshly ground black pepper to taste. Stir in the parsley.
5. Add the flaked fish and prawns and carefully stir together. Turn into a deep pie dish.
6. Drain the potatoes, mash and beat till creamy with a knob of butter and milk.
7. Top the fish mixture with the potato and mark with the back of a fork.
8. Place the dish on a baking tray to catch baking drips.
9. Bake at 350F, Gas 4, 180C for twenty five minutes till golden and bubbling and serve straight from the oven.

ORKNEY FUDGE CHEESECAKE

On Fire Alarm Day evening the food writers ended their adventure with dinner. A 100% endorsement of the Orkney fudge cheesecake resulted in Paul Doull sharing his recipe.

Serves 6 to 8 people
Takes 30 minutes to make
Melt on the hob or in a bowl in the microwave

You will need:-
1 x 200g pkt Hobnob Biscuits
1 x 200g pkt Digestive Biscuits
175g (6ozs) butter
450mls (15fl ozs) double cream
150g bar Orkney fudge
200g Plain Philadelphia cream cheese

To make:-
1. Put the biscuits into a thick polythene bag and crush with a rolling pin – make sure the bag is sealed!
2. Melt the butter in a large pan and then stir in the biscuit crumbs till moist.
3. Press into an oiled flan dish or ring about 20cm (8")' diameter. Chill to set.
4. Meanwhile make the filling. Whip the cream till softly stiff, beat the cream cheese till smooth and fold the two together.
5. Finally melt the Orkney fudge in a bowl over a pan of hot water or in the microwave in bursts of thirty seconds. Stir quickly into the cheese and cream mixture.
6. Pour onto the set biscuit base and chill to set.
7. Decorate with chocolate curls (see below) and swirls of piped cream
8. You can also make individual cheesecakes using ramekin dishes or plate rings as moulds.

CHOCOLATE CURLS

Use a curved surface – the inside of a halved new clean plastic drainpipe is ideal.
Taking a flat sheet of baking parchment or acetate film lay it flat on the worktop. Melt some good quality dark chocolate and pour a thin skin onto the parchment or film. Mark with the blade of a sharp knife into elongated triangles and immediately very carefully lift into the up turned half pipe. Leave to set. Remove from the film and store in an airtight box. Repeat to build up a store – very handy, and they look so professional.

IT'S BOUND TAE BE GOOD

Recent events have encouraged me to trace Orcadian family roots through my Great Grandfather's name of Cumming. Pointed in the direction of Kirkwall Library and the Orkney Family History Society I asked for assistance. I am so glad that I did and kicking myself for waiting so long.

Assisted by George Gray, Nan Scott and other stalwarts I soon found myself with armfuls of print outs on great, great grannies, great aunts, uncles and all sorts. I set off for Scotland to study the results. Imagine my excitement to read that one Great Grannie, from the island of Eday, was named Isabella 'Pitcairn' Loutit.

On discussing this with a well known Orcadian Man of Letters I learned that two of the famous 'Mutiny on the Bounty' crew had been Orcadian. Had one of these been my Great Grandfather? Knowing that some of the mutineers had settled on Pitcairn Island in the South Seas I even went so far as to send an email to the island's History Archives.

'There must be some truth in this, Liz,' my father suggested. 'No wonder we all love bananas.'

On the next visit to Orkney I eagerly anticipated telling all at OFHS about these exciting discoveries but - talk about slipping on a banana skin – one click of the computer mouse revealed that many children had been baptised on Eday with the same middle name, after William Pitcairn the local minister. So much for the bananas!

CHOCOLATE BOUNTIES

Thoughts of Pitcairn naturally revived memories of the famous Bounty Bar advert on TV. This recipe is a simple, no-cook version of the famous bar. Handy when relations come to call.

Makes up to 30
Takes 20 minutes to make
No baking needed

You will need:-
115g (4ozs) margarine
115g (4ozs) icing sugar
225g (8ozs) desiccated coconut
1 small tin of condensed milk
225g (8oz) dark chocolate to cover
Small paper cases

To make:-
1. Cream the margarine and icing sugar till light, add the condensed milk and coconut and mix well together.
2. Line a tray with foil and then using clean slightly wet hands roll the coconut mixture into balls the size of a small walnut and lay onto the tray.
3. Leave to set in a cool place for about one hour.
4. Melt the chocolate in a bowl over hot water or in the microwave on high power for one minute or until melted.
5. Lay thirty paper cases onto a tray to stand beside the bowl of melted chocolate.
6. Use a skewer to dip the little coconut bounty balls into the chocolate then gently nudge off the point with a knife into one of the paper cases. Repeat till all are coated.
7. Set in the fridge.

Cook's tip:-
Add a little rum or pina colada to the coconut mix.
Add a few chopped raisins to the mix.
There is always some left over chocolate in the bowl. Use to make Bounty Bananas.

BOUNTY BANANAS

Great on a hot day.

Serves 4 people
Takes 5 minutes to prepare and 1-hour freezer time.
No cooking needed

You will need:-
4 medium size bananas
115g (4ozs) chocolate of your choice, white, milk or plain

To make:-
1. Skin the bananas and cut into chunks about 5cm (2inches) long.
2. Insert a cocktail stick and open freeze on a plastic tray for 1 hour.
3. Break the chocolate into small pieces and put into a heat-proof bowl. Melt over a pan of hot water or in the microwave on full power on bursts of one minute till melted.
4. Serve the melted chocolate in a bowl with the frozen banana on a plate at the side.
5. Dip into melted dark chocolate and enjoy.

BANANA SPLITS

A great camp fire delicacy from Girl Guide Days.

Allow one banana per person.
Make a slit in the curve of the banana, prize open with clean fingers to fill with chopped marshmallows and strawberry jam.
Wrap in foil and bake in the fire, barbecue or oven.
Open the foil parcel taking care that the escaping steam does not scald bare skin.
Add a scoop of ice cream and enjoy.
Remember to put the 'foil dish' into the bin provided.

Patrol Leader's ideas:-
Add chopped mars bar, milky way, chocolate chips, fudge or toffee.
Maltesers for a less fattening centre!

THE FLYING DUTCHMAN

Tracing your roots must be catching for my cousin Sheila, a computer expert, has also caught the bug. Having secured a printed copy of our Great Grandfather Thomas Warren's Last Will and Testament dated 1844, Sheila was, to say the least, excited. He had died owed the modern equivalent of half a million pounds by Thomas Traill, a Dutch businessman, who had disappeared without trace.

On the strength of this discovery Sheila planned a trip to the Amsterdam Archives to find out more. 'You never know,' she told me. 'We might own some of the Dutch Bulb Fields.'

Who could this mysterious Dutchman be? Could I do some research on the islands, she asked, and find out about any Dutch connections with Orkney. Hot foot I went to the archives of Elgin Library where I found a copy of The Islands of Orkney by Liv Kjørsvik Schei, with photographs by the legendary Gunnie Moberg.

Avidly reading I discovered that a Dutch war ship, named the Utrecht, had been wrecked on Sanday in February 1807 during the Napoleonic Wars. The Captain and 366 survivors, from the crew of 450, surrendered to the local Laird. Some might have remained and integrated with the population. Could this be the missing link? 'Why,' I asked Sheila, 'do you think that Thomas Traill was Dutch?' 'Because the will says he came from Holland,' she replied.

This seemed conclusive until, at the Orkney Family History Society, I learned that there are many Orcadian farms called Holland, which means 'High Land'. Thomas Traill owned one such farm on Papa Westray, therefore Sheila and I had come to the obvious, but misguided, conclusion that he was Dutch. We lost our half million pounds but found instead a lovely book and had a good laugh at the same time.

HOT HONEY ROASTED ROOTS

Roots: tracing them, cooking them or both for just as plants have roots so do we. Emphasised by a recent comment on Radio Orkney, 'No matter where in the world you go there has usually been an Orcadian there before you!'

Serves 4 people
Takes ten minutes to prepare and 45 minutes to oven roast
Oven roast at 200C, 400F, Gas 6 on the middle shelf

You will need:-

2 large carrots peeled
1 medium turnip peeled
1 parsnip peeled
2 potatoes peeled
2 onions peeled
1 red pepper cored and de-seeded

For the coating
2 tablespoons runny honey
2 tablespoons light olive oil or sunflower oil
Sea Salt
Freshly ground black pepper
Chilli flakes

To make:-

1. Line a deep roasting tin with foil and preheat the oven to 400F, 200C, Gas 6.
2. Cut the carrot, turnip, parsnip and potato into rough chunks.
3. Add quarters of onion and some strips of red pepper.
4. Put into a large bowl with runny honey and light olive or sunflower oil and mix well together.
5. Put into the lined roasting tin and sprinkle lightly with chilli flakes.
6. Put into the middle of the pre-heated oven and roast for thirty to forty five minutes till tender and caramelised turning once after twenty minutes cooking time.
7. Season lightly with a sprinkle of sea salt and ground black pepper and serve hot with roasts and grills.

Cook's tip:-
Like Orcadian genealogy this dish has many roots.
Add chops or shredded chicken, cover with foil and oven bake.
Makes a great Spanish omelette or tortilla.
Serve hot honey roast roots with my friend Su's hot smoked paprika sauce.

SU'S HOT SMOKED PAPRIKA SAUCE

This simple sauce tastes great hot or cold, with pasta, meat or rice.

Here is how Su makes the tomato sauce.
You will need:-
1 medium onion peeled and finely chopped
1 tablespoon sunflower or grapeseed oil
0.5 level teaspoon smoked paprika, for a hotter
sauce add more
Balsamic vinegar
Red wine
Tomato Puree
1 tin chopped tomatoes in juice or equivalent of
passatta (225g [8ozs])
Sea salt

To make:-
1. Sweat the onion in oil till soft but not coloured stirring occasionally to prevent sticking.
2. Add smoked paprika, a glugg of balsamic vinegar and also red wine (plus some for the cook)
3. Add a squeeze of tomato puree and a tin of chopped tomatoes or carton of passatta.
4. Stir well, turn down the heat and simmer for ten minutes till thickened stirring occasionally.
5. Season with sea salt but you will find that just a very little is all that is needed.
6. Serve hot or cold as a sauce or dip.

THE WHASSIGO WEEKEND

Early one summer I was given the opportunity to house-sit for my Kirkwall cousins Ron and Fi while baking on Orkney. They returned from holiday late on the Saturday night, in time to enjoy another cousin, Hazel's, 60th birthday party the following day.

Hindsight, as they say, is a great thing. Therefore experience affords me the wisdom to declare that everyone, at some time in their lives, should attend an Orkney birthday party. We arrived in the late afternoon to eventually wend our way home some time after sunset, filled with all sorts of goodness and sore with laughter.

Nothing seemed more natural than Cousin Ron sallying into the kitchen to produce one of his impromptu feasts. He donned an apron and opened a bottle of Pinot Grigio to lubricate tired vocal chords. Almost immediately 'O Sole Mio' reverberated from the kitchen as delicious sizzling aromas wafted forth and, before we knew it - a whassigo!

In Orkney speak, according to baker Paul Groundwater, a 'whassigo' is something that happens on the spur of the moment, is fantastic but can never be repeated. Cousin Ron's impromptu feast was the first whassigo of the weekend.

Monday morning early, after a few blinks of sleep, I drove to Stromness to board the MV Hamnavoe for the crossing to Caithness. The ferry was literally humming with musicians returning home after the weekend of the Stromness Folk Festival. An enthusiastic young lad and his two friends went on deck to play us out of the harbour to the tune of Peter Maxwell Davies's Leaving Stromness on his fiddle. Before I knew it a host of other musicians with more fiddles, banjos and even a bodhran appeared on the sunlit deck.

As the Hamnavoe cruised through blue calm seas in grand musical style Strip the Willow, the Dashing White Sergeant, Kentucky Blue Grass and Ragtime filled the air. The dancers reeled and jigged, feet tapped and hands clapped to the music all the way to Scrabster. Even the crew joined in, blowing the ship's horn. It certainly was a whassigo and a half!

COUSIN RON'S WHASSIGO CHICKEN

Chef Ron donned an apron, opened a bottle of Pino Grigio to lubricate tired vocal cords; almost instantly O Sole Mio reverberated from the kitchen as delicious sizzlings and aromas wafted forth and before we knew it . . . . .

Serves 4 people
Takes as long as it takes depending how good the party is
Cook on the hob

You will need:-
4 medium boneless chicken breasts - skinned
2 eating apples, peeled cored and chopped, Cox or Braeburn are best.
1 ripe avocado pear , halved, stoned, skinned and chopped
1 large glass white wine. Open a bottle!
A handful of fresh garden herbs: thyme, bay, marjoram, parsley, sage. Use what is available.
Sea salt
Freshly ground black pepper
3 tablespoons long grain or basmati rice
2 tablespoons of frozen peas, sweet corn or mixed vegetables
Olive Oil
Crushed fresh garlic. Granules are a good alternative.

To make:-
1. Get the creative juices flowing and pour a glass of white wine. All good cooks ensure that ingredients are suitable for purpose. Thus inspired continue in full voice.
2. Heat a little olive oil in a deep frying pan and seal the chicken breasts.
3. Add the garlic, season with sea salt and ground black pepper. Stir in the fruit and avocado, pour in the wine and reduce the heat, cover the pan to simmer slowly.
4. Meanwhile boil the rice till tender adding the vegetables to cook for the last 5 minutes.
5. Drain the rice mixture, add to the chicken in the pan and stir together mixing all the juices.
6. Cook slowly for a few minutes to heat through and serve.
7. Best eaten late evening, shared with loved ones, while watching the lights of Kirkwall harbour flicker in the bay below.

WHASSIGO TWO: THE ORKNEY FUDGE FANCY

A reel blend of Orkneyness. I may never meet those musicians again, however, on the off chance that one or some of you read this: On behalf of every member of the passengers and crew, thank you. Those lusty musicians used a lot of energy, so, to fuel the fire and hopefully encourage a repeat I have created the Orkney Fudge Fancy.

You will need:-

350g (12ozs) plain flour
15mls (1 level tablespoon) baking powder
Pinch of salt
115g (4ozs) caster sugar
2 eggs, beaten
150 mls (0.25 pint) milk
50 mls (2 tablespoons) sunflower or corn oil
1 teaspoon ground cinnamon
1 eating apple peeled, cored and chopped
1 bar Orkney Fudge, chopped.
Chilling for about thirty minutes in the fridge makes chopping much easier.

Make 10 to 12 fancies
Takes 45 minutes to make
Oven bake at 190C, 375F,
Gas 5 on the middle shelf

To make:-

1. Turn on the oven to heat and line twelve deep muffin tins with paper muffin cases.
2. Sift the flour, baking powder, cinnamon and salt into a deep mixing bowl. Stir in the chopped apple and Orkney Fudge.
3. Beat the egg, oil and milk together in a bowl, add to the other ingredients and stir to make a soft batter.
4. Divide between the muffin cases and bake in the middle of the pre-heated oven for twenty five minutes till risen and golden.
5. Leave to cool a little in the tins, dust with a little icing sugar and eat warm.

Cook's tip:-

Drizzle with a little lemon water icing made by mixing icing sugar with fresh lemon juice. Use the back of a teaspoon to roughly coat the top of each cooled fancy. Eat while sticky.

CENTURIES OF MANSE FAMILIES

Houses, like people, have souls. Some live only a short time and return to the dust from which they came while others outlive the three score years and ten of mere mortals. As we grow and are changed by life's happenings so do those buildings.

Everyone needs somewhere to belong, where they feel safe and secure. From one bedroom flats to mansions and mud huts; the unique place which they call home. Sadly, some buildings lack warmth of welcome. They stand dark and foreboding giving little comfort to those under their roofs while, in contrast, there are those which gladly open their doors like arms to hug, shelter and nurture. Such a house stands on Westray.

The restored West Manse is built on a high cliff, silhouetted against the windy sky, looking out towards Nova Scotia. It casts a caring eye over Mae Sands below and further across the island towards Orkney's Mainland and Kirkwall shimmering in the distance.

For centuries wind and rain have beaten on the roof of this remarkable manse yet it remains firmly planted on solid rock. Neither the storms of climate nor of life have moved it since the first stone was laid in 1520. As I sat in the drawing room listening to the whooshing wind in the eves it seemed that the manse whispered in my ear.

'People are the most important thing to me. Time passes and the ways of Men change, but in the end it is what is in their hearts that matters. To contain and restore this love is why I was built and I pray that all those who are touched by my story will listen, learn and go forth more caring of their fellow man.'

FATTY CUTTIES

Not quite a biscuit, but certainly not a cake, fatty cutties are baked on a griddle and unique to Westray. Perhaps they resemble a luxurious Garibaldi but there the similarity ends. They are by themselves a 'Fatty Cuttie', and there is no one recipe for there are as many different fatty cutties as there are bakers on the island.

This quantity makes eighteen to twenty thin crisp fatty cutties.
Takes 30 minutes to make
Cook on a hot flat griddle plate or thick bottomed frying pan.

You will need:-
175g (6ozs) plain flour sifted with
a pinch of bicarbonate of soda
115g (4ozs) margarine
60g (2ozs) currants
60g (2ozs) caster sugar

To make:-
1. Put the margarine and sugar into a bowl and beat till soft and fluffy.
2. Add the flour, bicarbonate of soda and currants and mix to a soft dough.
3. Meanwhile put the griddle or thick bottomed frying pan to heat on low.
4. Turn the dough onto a floured board. Knead lightly together and form into an oblong. Cut into 3 pieces.
5. Taking each piece in turn, shake a little flour over the top and roll out thinly with a well floured rolling pin. Form into a thin even strip 10cm (4 inches) wide.
6. Cut across a strip into fingers about 3.25cm (1.5 inches) wide. You should get six or seven. Repeat with the other two dough pieces.
7. Test the temperature of the griddle or frying pan with a shake of flour. If the flour turns pale golden it is at the correct heat. Fatty cutties burn easily so it is essential to check the heat. I burnt my first batch!
8. Bake for 3 minutes on each side till pale golden, turning once with a palette knife or fish slice.
9. Cool on a wire rack and store in an airtight tin.

CRUNCHIE NOISES

Look under the stair at the West Manse to find the best of Dolls' Houses. An imaginary world which reminded me of a favourite childhood recipe my cousin Jennifer called Crunchie Noises. Why? Because they make such a noise inside your head as you eat them.

Makes an oiled rectangular Swiss Roll Tin 19cm x 28cm (7.5 inches x 11 inches)
Takes 30 minutes to make
Oven bake at 170C, 325F, Gas 3 on the middle shelf

You will need:-
5 Weetabix or similar cereal biscuits
225g (8ozs) porridge oats
75g (3ozs) soft brown sugar
2.5g (0.5 teaspoon) baking powder
115g (4ozs) soft margarine
15mls (1 tablespoon) golden syrup

To make:-
1. The easy way to prepare the baking tin is to paint the inside with a pastry brush (kept for the purpose) dipped in light cooking oil. Turn on the oven to heat.
2. Crumble the cereal biscuits into a bowl, add the porridge oats and baking powder and mix together.
3. Melt the golden syrup, sugar and margarine together in a pan or in a bowl in the microwave on high power for one to two minutes.
4. Add to the dry ingredients and stir together. Turn into the prepared baking tin and flatten using the back of a spoon dipped in hot water to prevent sticking.
5. Bake for fifteen minutes till set and golden. This recipe burns easily so keep watch!
6. Cool in the tin, marking into squares while still warm. Store in an airtight tin.

Cook's tips:-
Add a handful of raisins or sultanas. Better still some chocolate chips.
Ss . . . sh . . . sh . . . sh, crunch away no-one is listening below the West Manse stairs!

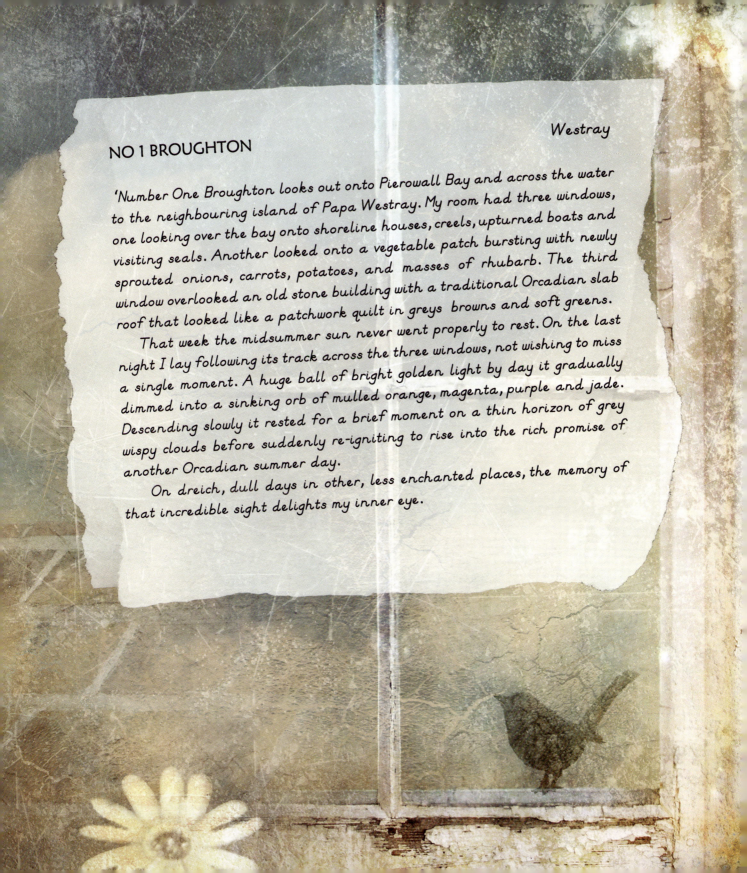

NO 1 BROUGHTON

'Number One Broughton looks out onto Pierowall Bay and across the water to the neighbouring island of Papa Westray. My room had three windows, one looking over the bay onto shoreline houses, creels, upturned boats and visiting seals. Another looked onto a vegetable patch bursting with newly sprouted onions, carrots, potatoes, and masses of rhubarb. The third window overlooked an old stone building with a traditional Orcadian slab roof that looked like a patchwork quilt in greys browns and soft greens.

That week the midsummer sun never went properly to rest. On the last night I lay following its track across the three windows, not wishing to miss a single moment. A huge ball of bright golden light by day it gradually dimmed into a sinking orb of mulled orange, magenta, purple and jade. Descending slowly it rested for a brief moment on a thin horizon of grey wispy clouds before suddenly re-igniting to rise into the rich promise of another Orcadian summer day.

On dreich, dull days in other, less enchanted places, the memory of that incredible sight delights my inner eye.

Breakfast at No 1 Broughton is deliciously different because the owner, Jerry Wood's mother is Finnish. He often serves his Finnish-Orcadian version of Karelian pastries for which he kindly gave me the recipe. Best eaten warm they also make a great any time snack.

KARELIAN PASTRY (Karjalan Piirakka)

Small ovals of pastry filled with a savoury rice mixture, egg washed and baked – serve warm.

Makes 12 to 14 pastries
Takes 1 hour to prepare and bake
Bake in a hot oven, Gas 8, 450F, 230C near the top of the oven

For the pastry you will need:-
75g (3ozs)-rye flour – you can use Orkney Bere meal instead
50g (2ozs) plain white flour
1 dessertspoon vegetable oil
Pinch of salt
Water to mix

For the filling:-
75g (3ozs) short grain pudding rice
1 pint milk or water
1 teaspoon salt
1 dessertspoon butter
Beaten egg to coat

To make:-
1. First make the filling by simmering the rice in the water or milk with the butter and salt till soft and thickened. This will take at least thirty minutes. Watch the rice and stir occasionally to prevent sticking. Leave to cool a little. Buttery mashed potatoes also make a good filling.
2. Turn on the oven to heat.
3. Make the pastry by mixing the ingredients with enough cold water to form stiff dough. Roll into a sausage shape about 5 cms (2 inches) thick and then cut into slices about 0.5 inch wide.
4. Take each slice of dough and roll it into an oval shaped ball in the palm of your hand. Then roll it thinly into an oval shape.
5. Spread filling into the middle of the oval leaving an edge of pastry to roll over and crimp by pinching with the thumb and forefinger so that it forms a sort of frill round about centre of rice or potatoes.
6. Lift onto a baking tray and brush the edges with beaten egg. Bake near the top of the oven for a scant ten minutes till golden on top.
7. Serve warm with pickled herring, grated cheese melted on top or the traditional egg butter.

EGG BUTTER

Easy, no cooking and serves four people.

To Make:-
1. Shell two large warm newly hardboiled eggs and chop finely.
2. Mix with plenty softened butter and season lightly with sea salt and ground black pepper.
3. Spoon onto the middle of a warm freshly baked Karelian pastry.

Cook's tip:-
Stir grated cheese into the rice or potato filling at step 2.
Any left-over pastries can be reheated under a grill or popped into the toaster on low.

PULLA

The fragrant baking aroma of this cardamom scented bread is mouth-watering.

Make in the bread maker to the sweet enriched dough recipe
500g (1lb) size of mix makes 1 loaf.
Oven bake at 190C, 375F, Gas 5 on the middle shelf.

You will also need:-
3 teaspoons roughly ground cardamom, easily ground from cardamom seeds using a coffee grinder or mortal and pestle ·
Caster sugar
Beaten egg
Flaked almonds

To make:-
1. Follow the sweet enriched dough recipe on your bread machine, adding the roughly ground cardamom to the ingredients.
2. Turn the dough out onto a floured surface, knead and roll into long sausage shape.
3. Cut along the length with sharp knife to make three even strips joined at one end.
Pleat the three strips together, lay on an oiled baking tray and put into a warm place for about thirty minutes to rise till almost doubled. Turn on the oven to heat.
4. Brush with beaten egg, sprinkle with caster sugar and flaked almonds. Bake for twenty five to thirty minutes till golden and hollow sounding when knocked on the base with the knuckles.
5. Cool on a wire tray. Best eaten newly baked and spread thickly with butter.

WHALE OF A FISH SLICE

The derelict West Manse has been restored as a retreat for aspiring cooks, writers and artists, given a new lease of life by William and Sandy McEwen who had already restored the old mill at Trenaby. After long months of advertising the derelict manse was still without a buyer and the Westray community persuaded the semi-retired McEwens to have another go. Many people assisted and I was asked to help in kitchen related matters.

The island of Westray is an archaeological treasure trove and a research team from Edinburgh, also involved in the restoration, return each summer. During one annual dig while I was on coffee making duties, in the shell of what is now a fabulous kitchen, a 'digger' entered clutching what looked like a modern, plastic fish slice. Perfectly shaped with an easy to grip handle and sensibly angled slotted, flat lifting part he had found it lying in mud at the bottom of a roadside ditch. After a wash and rinse in the sink it became apparent that this was no Habitat purchase from the sixties, but expertly carved from whalebone and, indeed, it proved to be of Neolithic origin.

Since then many amazing finds have been announced, not least the small statue Christened 'Westray Venus'. I wonder if she was a Neolithic housewife who wielded just such a fish slice as she cooked fish and chips for her family.

KING SCALLOPS WITH LEEK AND GINGER

The Westray Venus would most certainly have served fish to her family but not with chips. No tatties on Orkney when she wielded her fish slice. However, there was, without doubt, a plentiful supply of seafood which she probably cooked on hot stones at the side of the fire. Christopher Trotter created this recipe.

Serves 4 people
Takes 10 minutes to prepare and cook
Cook on the hob

You will need:-
16 to 20 scallops trimmed and washed
2 leeks
2.5cm (1inch) root ginger
Light olive oil
30g (1oz) butter
130mls (1/4) pint fish stock
75mls (2 fl ozs) double cream or 30g (1oz) butter

To make:-
1. Trim and wash the leeks and cut into thin strips about 10cm (4inches) long.
2. Peel and cut the ginger into fine strips.
3. Heat the butter and a little olive oil in a frying pan and then sear the scallops on both sides, allowing them to colour slightly.
4. Remove from the pan and keep warm. Add the leek and stir to lightly brown. Allow to go limp.
5. Add the ginger and season with a little sea salt.
6. To make a sauce add the fish stock to the leek and ginger mixture, reduce and swirl in butter or cream to thicken.
7. Taste and adjust the seasoning if needed, then pour over the scallops to serve.

POWER CUT SPECIAL

During the winter power cut year of 1969 another 'by the side of the fire' recipe evolved out of necessity. My mother cleverly devised a way of baking this dish in the oven till the power went off and completed its cooking at the side of the open fire. We loved our fire side candlelit meals, lots of chat, laughter. No telly either.

Serves 4 people
Takes as long as it takes when there is no power and an open fire
Or 20 minutes to prepare and 2 hours to cook
Oven cook at 160C, 325F, Gas 3 on the middle shelf

You will need:-
550g (1.25lb) lean steak mince
Sea Salt
Ground Black Pepper
2 onions peeled and finely sliced
2 sticks celery chopped
225g (8oz) can of chopped tomatoes
Generous squirt of tomato puree
1 teaspoon Worcester sauce
150mls (0.25 pint) water
Light cooking oil

To make:-

1. Turn on the oven to heat.
2. Season the mince with a little sea salt and ground black pepper and then shape into eight fat burgers.
3. Heat a little oil in a frying pan and quickly brown the burgers on both sides. Remove from the pan and put into a deep casserole dish.
4. Toss the vegetables into the frying pan and soften a little in the juices stirring continuously.
5. Scatter over the burgers.
6. Lastly heat the tomatoes, puree and Worcester sauce in the frying pan and stir in the water to make a sauce. Bring to the boil then pour over the ingredients in the casserole dish.
7. Cover and put into the oven to cook for two hours.
8. Bake potatoes beside the casserole for the last hour.
9. Before serving the casserole taste the sauce and adjust the seasoning.

Cook's tip:-

Add sliced mushrooms, carrots and or chopped red pepper to the vegetable mix.
Continues to cook at the side of the fire, on a wood burning stove or similar.
Ironically this dish freezes well too.

CENTENARY CELEBRATION

Perched on the hill above Stromness stands St. Peter's House, which began life as a bustling manse. By the early 1950s it was no longer in use but Gordon Robertson, Director of Social Welfare, dreamt of providing a home here for the elderly. Officially opened in 1957 by the famous local artist Stanley Cursiter it continues to fulfil both men's vision and, as such, it was host to a special birthday on 14th June 2009.

This was the day that Kathleen Firth became 100 years old. Born in the Welsh capital, Cardiff, in 1909 her family moved to London where she grew up. It was there that she met and married Orcadian pharmacist Nicol Firth and, soon after, returned with him to his home in Stromness. Together they ran the local Hamnavoe Pharmacy until Nicol's death in 1978. She continued to live an independent life until becoming a resident in St. Peter's House at the age of 98.

Two years later an action packed day celebrated her Centenary. While making plans her son Howie discovered a long lost school friend, Stewart McConnach, now a well known Caithness baker. In honour of the occasion Stewart produced a Centenary Biscuit labelled with a picture of their childhood homes on the harbourside at Stromness.

The birthday began with a family drive to Skara Brae for lunch after which Kathleen returned to a flower bedecked St. Peter's House for a nap. Thus restored, she greeted her guests in the conservatory while sipping a glass of chilled champagne. Unfortunately a foot injury prevented Stewart attending the soiree but he sent telephone greetings to which Kathleen replied, 'I remember the pair of you breeding hamsters in the bedroom'. Some memory, because the last time Kathleen saw Stewart he had been only ten years old.

Later, a home cooked St. Peter's Birthday Buffet was served in the dining room where she held court as guest of honour, feet tapping to music played by friend Jean Leonard and her young musicians, joining in now and again with the words of a weel kent air.

LAVERNE'S FUDGE

Kathleen is partial to more than the odd nibble of Orkney fudge so Laverne Stanger, one of Kathleen's caring nurses, makes a regular supply for the centenarian. She has kindly shared her special recipe so here it is for you to make and enjoy.

Makes a slab approximately 28cm x 18cm (11inches x 7inches)
Takes 1 hour to make
Cook on the hob

You will need:-
900g (2lbs) granulated sugar
225g (8ozs) butter
200mls (7fl ozs) milk
1 tin condensed milk
4 drops vanilla essence

To make:-
1. Prepare a tin or tray by painting with a pastry brush dipped in sunflower or vegetable oil to prevent the fudge sticking.
2. Put sugar, butter and the milk into a pan and stir continuously over a medium heat to dissolve the sugar.
3. Keep stirring till the mixture is boiling, then boil for fifteen minutes.
4. Add the condensed milk and stir till the mixture is boiling once more.
5. Keep stirring as the mixture boils until it begins to change colour. Add the vanilla essence and stir while boiling.
6. Test a drop in a cup of cold water. When a hard ball is formed it is ready to pour.
7. Cool a little stirring all the time, then pour into an oiled tin to set.
8. Mark while warm and cool in the tin.

IRYNA'S BLUEBERRY CAKE

December 2009 Howie Firth travelled to St Peter's in Stromness to join mother Kathleen for her 100th Christmas and 100th New Year. Exchange student friend, Iryna from Ukraine, made a cake recipe from her country for Kathleen and she loved it, which proves that you are never too old to try something new.

Makes a cake 20cm (8inches) round cake tin
Takes 1 hour to make
Oven bake at 200C, 400F, Gas 6

You will need:-
3eggs
300g (10 ozs) caster sugar
500g (1lb 2ozs) plain flour
2.5 teaspoons baking powder
1.5 teaspoons vanilla sugar or
1 teaspoon vanilla essence
150g (5.5ozs) melted butter
150mls (0.25pt) double cream whipped
115g (4ozs) fresh blueberries washed a dried

To make:-
1. Turn on the oven to heat at 200C, 400F, Gas 6. Oil and line a cake tin.
2. Whisk the eggs with the sugar till thick and holding the trail of the whisk.
3. Sift the flour, baking powder and vanilla sugar (if using) into a bowl.
4. In a separate bowl mix the melted butter with the whipped cream.
5. Fold the flour and butter mixture into the whipped egg and sugar then pour into a prepared cake tin.
6. Scatter the top of the cake with blueberries.
7. Bake in the middle of the oven for forty five to fifty minutes till risen and the point of a skewer inserted in the middle of the cake comes out clean.
8. Cool in the tin, wrap in foil and store in a cool place in an airtight tin.
9. Eat within one week. Delicious served with more fresh blueberries and whipped cream.

Cook's Tip
Whisk the eggs and sugar in a bowl over a pan of hot water which will cook the eggs slightly, helping to trap more air which makes a lighter cake.

DIAMONDS ARE FOREVER

Traditionally sixty years is marked as a diamond anniversary which my parents celebrated on 14th April 2008. However, it is a little known fact that another diamond celebration coincided with theirs, that of the reopening of Highland Park Distillery after its being closed during the Second World War. Interestingly, my father played an important part in both.

Keen to introduce his new wife to Orcadian roots the groom arranged a flight on one of the first passenger planes from Aberdeen, to spend a fortnight's honeymoon based in the Kirkwall Hotel.

During their stay a business man, his wife and young daughter arrived and it transpired that his mission was to reinstate Highland Park Distillery which had been out of production during the war. He kindly invited my father to accompany him on his first visit when they not only turned the key in the lock but also a cork of Highland Park, to enjoy a dram, to toast my parent's wedding and the future success of the distillery.

That dram of Highland Park began two very different journeys whose roads have converged six decades later. My parents built a life full of love, three daughters, a grandson, and many friendships. Highland Park in a different way followed the same values of positive hard work and enthusiasm.

Sixty years later, while working on Orkney, I contacted Pat Retson, the Brand Heritage Manager and, as a result Highland Park was delighted to take part once more in wedding celebrations. Distillery Manager Russell Anderson who remembered my father from his early years in Moray, re-established the connection when he travelled from Orkney to present my parents with a bottle of 18 year old single malt to mark the double Diamond Anniversary.

Like diamonds childhood food memories last a lifetime and beyond. My sister and I had little difficulty remembering quite a cluster from which we chose:-

BACORN FLAN

In the late 1950's a group of wives from the neighbourhood joined the Women's Electrical Association, attending meetings to learn how to wire plugs, change fuses and use the latest electrical gadgets. Once they had a cookery demonstration given by Joan Peters, home economist to Britain's Pig Industry Development Authority. Mum's version of Joan's bacorn flan is so good that she has to make extra to meet the demand.

Makes a flan 20cm (8inches) in diameter
Takes 1 hour to prepare and bake
Oven bake at 190C, 375F, Gas 5 on the middle shelf

You will need:-
175g (6ozs) plain flour
85g (3ozs) margarine
Sea salt

For the filling:-
1 tin sweetcorn drained
115g (4ozs) chopped bacon
0.25 cup milk
2 eggs
Sea salt and ground black pepper
Worcester sauce
60g (2ozs) grated cheddar cheese
1 tomato sliced

To make:-
1. Turn on the oven to heat.
2. Place the pastry ingredients in a bowl. Rub in the margarine and mix to a stiff pliable dough with cold water.
3. Turn the pastry onto a floured board, knead smooth and roll out in a circle the diameter of the flan plus the depth of the sides. Lower into the flan dish or ring using a bent index finger to ease into the sides. Trim the edges with a sharp knife.
4. Mix the drained sweetcorn and bacon and spread over the pastry case.
5. Beat the milk and eggs together, season with sea salt, ground black pepper and Worcester sauce and pour over sweetcorn and bacon.
6. Scatter the grated cheese on top then arrange the sliced tomato in an attractive pattern over the cheese.
7. Bake for thirty five minutes till golden and bubbling. Serve hot or cold.

Cook's tip:-
Add chopped red pepper instead of bacon to serve to vegetarians.

SUGARY SHORTBREAD

The weekly bake had to include sugary shortbread which was kept, although not for long, in a large blue, enamel tin. This tin travelled many a time to Hopeman beach where sugary shortbread was a vital part of the necessary 'chittery bite' urgently required after bathing in the North Sea.

Makes 12 to 14 biscuits
Takes 1 hour to mix and bake
Oven bake at 180C, 350F, Gas
4 on the middle shelf

You will need:-
115g (4ozs) porridge oats
115g (4ozs) plain flour
85g (3ozs) caster sugar
75g (2.5ozs) margarine
60g (2ozs) white vegetable fat
1 teaspoon baking powder
2 drops of vanilla essence
Pinch of salt
Caster sugar to shake over the baked shortbread

To make:-
1. Turn on the oven to heat.
2. Cream the margarine, vegetable fat and sugar till light and fluffy.
3. Sift the flour, salt and baking powder into the mixture and add the vanilla essence and porridge oats.
4. Mix together till a clean ball of dough is formed.
5. Turn onto a floured work top, shake some flour on top and roll out to a rectangle 7.5cm (3inches) wide and 0.5cm (0.25 inch) thick.
6. Pinch round the edges with your thumb and forefinger to pattern the edges.
7. Prick the dough with a fork then cut into fingers 1cm (0.5 inch) wide.
8. Lift onto a baking tray with a palette knife or fish slice and bake in the middle of the oven for twenty minutes till pale golden and crisp.
9. Shake caster sugar over the hot shortbread on the tray. The sugar will stick to the hot biscuits while the tray catches the excess.
10. Lift onto a wire rack to cool and store in an airtight tin.

Cook's tip:-
An easy way to sprinkle sugar is to fill a teaspoon and hold it in your left hand to move slowly over the shortbread while gently tapping the side with your right forefinger.

HIGHLAND PARK PAGODA
Elgin and Highland Park Distillery, Kirkwall

A secret garden captured my childhood imagination. Every day as I returned from school I would stand on tiptoe to peer through the dark wooden bars of a heavy gate into a paradise garden bursting with fragrance and colour. This garden surrounded an imposing mansion built of sandstone, its grand baronial front door studded with big black nails.

One day in early spring I found the gate open. Dare I? One tentative step was followed by another – and yet another – until my eyes were almost popping. I must have stood for quite a time before a lovely lady appeared beside me. So began a friendship between this little girl and the beautiful woman whom I now know was the young wife of famous architect Charles Doig.

Mrs Doig invited me to tea, through the heavy doors and into a wonderland of oriental finery: Chinese urns, elephant feet filled with umbrellas and walking sticks, skins from tigers who looked very upset, silk fans and enormous paintings of faraway places. Best of all were the crystal door knobs which, on a sunny day, threw rainbows around the walls and onto the deeply padded, strangely shaped settees. Always the aroma of exotic spices filled the air; I loved my visits to Mrs Doig.

To me her husband was a rather distant figure of grandeur and learning, a kindly, elderly man who knew a great deal, it seemed, about everything. Time passed and in the natural way of things my visits ended.

Half a century later, during a whisky lecture at the Orkney International Science Festival, I learned that Highland Park whisky owes its world beating qualities to the unique Pagoda design of the distillery chimney – and who invented it? Charles Doig.

HIGHLAND PARK SUSHI

A Japanese sushi making set was given to me in a gift this Christmas. Snowed in and unable to join Hogmanay festivities, my son Alan and I used what we had in the house and invented 'Highland Park Sushi'.

Makes up to 30 rolls
Takes 1 hour to prepare and assemble
Cook the rice on the hob.

You will need:-
150g (5.5ozs) sushi rice
Highland Park 12 year old single malt whisky
Sea Salt
Light Soy sauce
Orkney smoked salmon
Savoy cabbage leaves

To make:-

1. Measure the rice into a bowl, cover with plenty cold water and stir briskly. Drain, repeat till the water runs clear.
2. Put the rice into a pan with a tight fitting lid and cover with 175mls (6fl ozs) cold water.
3. Put the lid on the pan and heat to boil. Do not lift the lid.
4. You will hear the water begin to boil, reduce the heat to continue simmering another five to 7 minutes.
5. Turn off the heat, do not lift the lid, leave the rice for ten minutes to cook in the steam.
6. Turn the rice into a bowl, stir in Highland Park Malt whisky and a little sea salt to taste. The recommended sugar is not required as the whisky gives such a mellow flavour.
7. Blanch trimmed outer leaves of the cabbage in boiling water for three to four minutes till limp. Refresh in cold water and drain well.
8. Cut the smoked salmon into thin strips ready to place on the rice.
9. Dry the cabbage between two layers of kitchen towel and roll flat with a rolling pin.
10. Put a rolling mat on to a chopping board and lay a cabbage leaf flat onto the mat.
11. Wet your hands a little and take a handful of the prepared rice, make a sausage shape and spread the rice evenly over the cabbage leaving a margin of 1cm (0.5inch) at the far edge of the leaf.
12. Use your index finger to make a hollow line for the smoked salmon. If liked you can smear a little wasabi paste along the pencil line channel then add a line of fish.
13. Lift the edge of the rolling mat to fold the leaf over the filling while you hold the fish in place with the tip of your fingers till the two edges of rice meet.
14. Remove your fingers and lift the edge of the mat over so that the cabbage leaf edges meet together.
15. Cover the roll with the mat and gently press to even and firm.

16. Dip a sharp knife in boiling water to prevent the rice sticking and cut the roll in half.
17. Lay the roll pieces parallel and cut into four, giving eight pieces of sushi.

Sushi Dips

1. 12 or 15 year old Highland Park single malt
2. Light soya sauce
3. Wasabi mayonnaise, easily made by mixing a small amount of wasabi powder or paste with a pinch of ground ginger and mayonnaise to taste.

Cook's tip:-

No wasabi? Mix horseradish sauce with mayonnaise, a little ground ginger and a pinch of chilli powder to taste.

KAREN'S CHOCAHOLIC FIX

Invented by Karen who works in the office at Highland Park Distillery, the staff, when asked for tasting comments replied 'it's addictive.' It never lasts long even when kept in the fridge.

Fills a large Swiss roll tin
Takes 10 minutes to make
Melting needed but no cooking. Use the Hob or microwave to melt the chocolate.

You will need:-
1 large jar of crunchy peanut butter
1 large block of white cooking chocolate
1 large packet off mini marshmallows

To make:-
1. Melt the chocolate in a bowl over a pan of hot water or in the microwave. Watch, the chocolate may burn in the microwave so process in bursts of 30 seconds till melted.
2. Mix together with the peanut butter then quickly stir in the marshmallows.
3. Scrape into an oiled Swiss roll tin or similar tray and put into the fridge.
4. Cut into squares and enjoy.

Cooks tip:-
It tastes much better chilled so keep in the fridge.
Use milk or plain chocolate instead of white.
Broken biscuits, dried fruit, add what you like, never the same twice.

SOWING SEEDS FOR THE FUTURE

In October 2005, Orkney general and agricultural seeds merchant Richard Shearer read an article in the Shetland Times written by Pete Glanville, Secretary of the Shetland Organic Producers Group. This was about Michael Johnstone, an Organic Farmer from Keith, whose Scandinavian wife had helped to source the seeds of an early ripening Finnish spring wheat named Anniina, which he had successfully grown for a number of years. Pete was keen to try the crop and sowed a small amount on a corner of his Shetland Farm that June. The Finnish Anniina wheat grew amazingly well to yield a small hand-gathered harvest early that autumn.

Thanks to five generations of family experience Richard realised that here was the possibility of growing an earlier ripening crop and so bring the harvest forward to avoid the inevitably cold and wet Orcadian autumn. That winter Richard did his homework and, the following March, brought home seeds of both Finnish Aniina wheat and Fiia oat. He approached the Agronomy Institute at Orkney College UHI asking for help to grow trial plots of the grains which they did with great success.

By 2009 Aniina Wheat and Fiiaa oats were being successfully grown on the islands and plans being made to trial higher protein Scandinavian wheat, suitable for bread making, and even earlier cropping Scandinavian oats as well as a malting Barley for Highland Park Distillery.

Oats are a superfood. However, within the oat world are many different varieties which, like us humans, behave very differently. For Orkney's northerly situation Fiiaa oats are, so far, the most promising. Easily grown they provide an abundant yield, are good to dry and mill. Full of flavour and nutritional goodness they are a dream to bake with.

MEALIE TATTIES

Since 1857, William Shearer has been the source of many an Orkney seed tattie. That unbeatable spud poetically described by tattie gourmet Richard Shearer in the annual seed catalogue, 'There can be nothing finer than the taste of the new season's tatties, their outer garments retained, boiled in sea water and buttered to taste'.

Serves 4 to 6 people
Takes 30 minutes to prepare and cook
Cook on the hob

You will need: -
1.5kg (3lb approx.) New Orkney tatties – Duke of York or Sharpes Express are a favourite.
1 tablespoon Medium freshly stone ground oatmeal – Barony Mill Orkney oatmeal F2 or F3 if available.
Sea Salt

To make:-
1. Scrub the fresh new potatoes and simmer in salted water till tender.
2. Drain well and steam.
3. Sprinkle with oatmeal, shake well to coat and serve.
4. Some folk add a knob of butter or a little bacon fat or dripping to melt and coat the potatoes before adding the oatmeal.

GREISEAGAN

A sweet skirlie originally made from suet, oatmeal and hedgerow berries, stirred in a pot, and hung on a hook called a cruik over the fire.
Takes five minutes not so much a recipe as a toss-it-in the pan pudding or quick hot breakfast.

Pour one tablespoon of sunflower oil into a pan and heat. Add a cup of medium oatmeal or oat flakes and two handfuls of currants and stir continuously till heated through. Serve hot with ice cream as a pudding, as a hot or cold meusli at breakfast or stirred into yoghurt for a healthy snack.

ORKNEY FUARAG

An ancient dish not unlike the famous Scottish crannachan, fuarag can be eaten as pudding or sweet spread on oatcakes, bannocks and scones.

Makes enough for 4
Takes 15 minutes to make. Best made in advance, preferably the day before.
Cook under the grill

You will need:-
60g (2ozs) medium oatmeal Barony Mill Oatmeal No 3
300mls (0.5pt) crowdie cheese, thick soured cream or similar
1 tablespoon runny Orkney honey or soft brown sugar

To make:-
1. Spread the oatmeal onto a baking tray and toast lightly under the grill at medium heat.
2. Put into a bowl with the cheese, honey or sugar and stir together.
3. Chill in the fridge at least one hour to allow the oatmeal to swell and thicken.
4. Serve as a cold dessert with fresh fruit in season. Wonderful with stewed rhubarb.
5. Serve as a spread accompanied by jam on pancakes, bannocks, oatcakes and scones. Rhubarb and ginger jam is a winner as are sliced fresh strawberries in season.

Cook's Tip:-
For a special occasion soak 60g (2ozs) raisins with 1 tablespoon 12 year old Highland Park Malt Whisky and a small piece of cinnamon stick overnight. Remove the cinnamon and add to the Fuarag at step 2.
Add fresh soft fruit in season at Step 2 to make an easy summer dessert.

BARONY MILL

Watermills have operated at Boardhouse since about 1500, the third of which was begun in 1872 by a local farming cooperative. Being the largest building in the area it was also used for weddings and dances. Homebrew and many a Bride's Cog fuelled exuberant dancing which caused a problem when the walls began to bulge outwards and as a consequence, metal rods and plates had to be installed.

At this point please bear in mind that the miller was required to buy his own stones and that his annual salary was only £12. French imported stones were desirable but proved very expensive at a massive £33 each. More affordable stones were sourced from Clackmannan at a still high £24. A softer local stone, suitable for bere meal, came from Yesnaby in Sandwick at a more affordable £12.

Transportation by horse and cart was impossible because the stones outweighed the horses and hoisted them off the ground. Instead, a long pole was inserted through the hole at the centre of the millstone so that it could be pulled by a garron, a sturdy Scottish work horse, with three men holding the pole on either side, guiding, pushing and lifting as required. Downhill without brakes proved a challenge more than once since a rolling stone tends to gather momentum if not moss.

Setting the millstones is a time consuming, highly skilled job carried out by the miller and his apprentice, adjusting screws in the floor which control the stone's height and thus the coarseness of the milled meal. The present mill was opened in 1873 and was in more or less constant use until 1998 when Birsay Heritage Trust refurbished the premises. Now known as the Barony Mill it continues under the management of the present miller, Rae Phillips, grandson of the man who took charge in 1910.

The success of the island grain project has resulted in increased demand for the services of the mill, processing the Scandinavian Annina wheat and Fiiaa oats. But, through all the changes in farming one grain has been constantly present, bere meal, ground from an ancient form of barley grown in Orkney since Neolithic times. This meal, with its distinctive taste and wholesome appearance, is traditionally used to bake the unleavened flat round bread called bere bannock. It is now also added to other commercially produced bakery products.

The mill's dancing shoes are still on its feet to 'Strictly Come Dancing' the moment the lade sluice is opened. The intricate wooden system comes alive to tango, samba and rock and roll to the beat of the water.

In earlier times our ancestors baked hearth cakes of grain on hot stones they had placed in a ring around the fire. The Gaels called these stones 'greadeal', hence the name of the round baking plates that modern Scots call a 'girdle'. This was invented and manufactured in the burgh of Culross, Fife where, in 1599, James VI granted the exclusive manufacturing rights to the burgh, endorsed by Charles II in 1666. Over the five centuries that milling has taken place at Boardhouse a sizeable proportion of the milled grain must have landed in one shape or form on a girdle known by Orcadians as a yetleen.

BERE MEAL BANNOCKS

A bannock is a round flat unleavened form of bread, which is baked on a girdle. Methods are consistent through most recipes. A bannock is often cut into triangles called 'farls' to share. This recipe comes from retired postman Johnny Johnston, who recommends 'consume with copious amounts of ale plus plenty of Orkney butter and cheese.'

Makes 2 or 3 round bannocks
Takes 30 minutes to prepare and bake
Bake on a Girdle or thick-bottomed frying pan
as for Blaanda Bread.

You will need:-
2 cups Barony Mills bere meal
1 cup plain flour
1 teaspoon bicarbonate of soda
1 teaspoon cream of tartar
Pinch of salt
Milk, water or buttermilk to mix.

To mix:-
1. Sift the dry ingredients into a bowl and mix to stiff dough with water, milk or buttermilk.
2. Turn out onto a board sifted with a mixture of flour and bere meal, half and shape each into a round flat bannock about 25mm (1 inch) thick.
3. Test the heat of the girdle with a sprinkle of flour, if it turns golden the heat is correct, pale too cold, burnt and it is to hot.
4. When the temperature is correct shake off the testing flour and lay the bannock on the surface. Bake four or five minutes till golden then turn to bake the other side.
5. The bannock is cooked through if it sounds hollow when knocked gently in the middle with the knuckles.
6. Cool in a clean tea towel on a wire tray. Enjoy warm and newly baked.

Postie's tip:-
Practice will make perfect.

MARGARET PHILLIPS'S BERE MEAL SCONES

The miller Rae Phillips's wife Margaret bakes excellent bere meal scones for which she kindly gave me this recipe.

Make 8 triangle scones
Takes 30 minutes to prepare and bake
Oven bake at 200C, 400F, Gas 6 on a shelf above the middle of the oven.

You will need:-
1.5 cups Bere meal
1 cup self-raising flour
1 tablespoon golden syrup
1 teaspoon bicarbonate of soda
0.5 teaspoon cream of tartar
0.5 Teaspoon Sea salt
60g (2ozs) margarine
1 cup butter milk

To make:-
1. Turn on the oven to heat and oil a baking tray.
2. Put all the dry ingredients into a bowl, rub in the margarine then add the buttermilk and mix to soft dough.
3. Turn onto a floured board and divide in two. Knead each into a ball and roll into a round 13mm (0.5 inch) thick. Cut each round into four triangles and put onto the baking tray.
4. Bake ten minutes till risen and lightly browned.
5. Cool in a clean tea towel on a wire tray and eat warm.

FULL CIRCLE

J F Groundwater, Baker and Greengrocer, began in 1914 when the present owner Paul's Great Great Grandfather, James Farquhar Groundwater bought Cursiter Brothers Bakery in Albert Street, Kirkwall, for his baker sons John and Jim. John's son, Jackie, then took over, passing the business in turn to his own son Harvey. Now Harvey's son Paul is in charge with the sixth generation, Michael and Daniel, already baking with Dad in the school holidays.

On 3rd December 2007 the Agronomy Team from Orkney College UHI, Paul and I began the adventure of determining whether the Finnish grains could have a commercial future on the islands. What a day we had, running our hands through a grain we knew instinctively was special and more than good. The aroma when we opened the first sack told us as much. With a raw ingredient which was so good in the first place, and which had been so expertly milled, we had the easy and best job producing many fabulous biscuits, breads and bannocks.

Within four days we had produced a selection of 28 different sweet and savoury biscuits and breads, our efforts culminating in a Taste and Try assessment kindly hosted in Lynnfield Hotel by our hotelier friend Malcolm Stout. We invited as many food folk as possible and, I am glad to say, opinion unanimously endorsed the potential of the grains.

That day my young friend Daniel came along to help. Quickly bored with adult conversation he was soon at a loose end until, on the spur of the moment, I suggested, 'Draw a mill wheel with all the grains of Orkney on it', and now thanks to this clever lad we have our new Orkney Grain logo.

ORKNEY OATMEAL OATCAKES

F. Marian McNeill describes enjoying oatcakes with herrings, sardines, cheese, curds, buttermilk, broth or kail, OR spread with butter and marmalade at breakfast. I am sure she would have loved the oatcakes Paul and I baked made with home grown Orkney Oatmeal.

Makes sixteen triangle oatcakes or farls
Takes 45 minutes to prepare and bake
Oven bake at 180C, 350F, Gas 4 in the top half of the oven

You will need:-
115g (4ozs) Barony Mill Orkney stoneground Medium oatmeal (no 3)
60g (2ozs) Barony Mill Orkney stoneground fine oatmeal (F 1)
0.25 level teaspoon sea salt
Pinch of bicarbonate of soda
30g (1 oz) vegetable margarine

To make:-
1. Turn on the oven to heat.
2. Put all the dry ingredients into a bowl and rub the margarine into the oatmeal.
3. Mix to a stiff pliable clean dough with warm water.
4. To prevent the dough sticking to the board use fine oat meal to roll out thinly. Divide the dough in half and roll each into a round ball. Roll into thin circles with a rolling pin. Cut each into eight triangles (or farls) and lay on an oiled or non-stick baking tray.
5. Bake fifteen minutes till crisp and curled. Cool on a wire tray and store in an airtight tin.

Cook's tip:-
Any similar stone-ground oatmeal can be used. Each will impart its own flavour and texture. Oatmeal burns easily, watch during baking and turn the baking trays to ensure even browning if needed.

PAUL GROUNDWATER'S ORKNEY BROONIE

Groundwater's Kirkwall Bakery was formerly the offices of Todd's Shipping business where my great grandfather worked before moving with his family to Leith. No wonder I feel at home there. This is Paul's recipe for traditional Orkney Broonie; a rich dark moist gingerbread cake. He also bakes the famous Highland Park Orkney Broonie created in memory of F. Marian McNeill.

Makes 3 x 375g (12ozs) broonies
Takes 1.5 hour to prepare and bake
Oven bake at 160C, 325F,
Gas 3 on the middle shelf.

You will need:-
350g (12ozs) plain flour or a mix of 50% Orkney Stoneground wheat flour and 50% Bread flour
115g (4ozs) medium oatmeal
115g (4ozs) soft brown sugar
115g (4ozs) margarine
85g (3ozs) golden syrup
85g (3ozs) black treacle
1 teaspoon bicarbonate of soda
1 teaspoon ground ginger
0.25teaspoon mixed spice
0.125 teaspoon chilli powder
60g (3ozs) raisins
Milk to mix

To make:-
1. Turn on the oven to heat. Oil the loaf tins by painting the inner surface with a pastry brush dipped in cooking oil, line the base with a strip of greaseproof paper, oil this too.
2. Sift the dry ingredients into a bowl, add the margarine and rub in till the mixture resembles fine breadcrumbs. Stir in the raisins.
3. Melt the syrup and treacle in a pan, warm don't boil.
4. Add to the dry ingredients, rinse out the stickiness from pan with warm water and then mix to a soft dropping consistency with milk.
5. Divide between the prepared tins. Lift onto a baking tray and bake for 30 to 40 minutes on the middle shelf of a preheated oven till risen, firm, and the point of a skewer inserted in the middle comes out cleanly.
6. Cool in the tins. Wrap in foil and store in an airtight tin.

Cook's tip:-
Add dried cranberries or sultanas instead of raisins.
Orkney wheat produces a soft flour low in gluten so Paul recommends 50/50 mix with stronger bread flour when baking cakes or bread.

ORKNEY INTERNATIONAL SCIENCE FESTIVAL

The Orkney Grain Project featured in the Festival of 2008 and during the planning stages Festival Director Howie Firth kindly gave me the opportunity to season that year with traditional Orkney food. With overwhelming island support there began a sharing of tradition with a difference, the warmth of Orcadian hospitality for those 'fae sooth and beyond'.

'Why toast always lands butter side down' launched the programme in typically light hearted fashion, although this year I am sure our toast fell butter side up to be topped with many varied layers.

The Orkney Grain Project Lecture and buffet lunch of home grown grain, breads, bannocks and biscuits washed down with Orkney Bere beer.

The men and women of the Firth Community Association served 167 high teas in two hours when it felt as if the entire island had come to visit. Like Jack Sprat and his wife they licked the platter clean leaving only one tattie and a box of millionaire's shortbread.

'Pizza the Fun' - making pizzas out of bannocks and making posh porridge at the family days.

Tastings and bake days with the children at local primary schools.

The daily opportunity to enjoy a scenic view of Kirkwall and Westray crab lunches in Lynnfield Hotel.

North Ronaldsay Suppers at the St Magnus Centre with homemade tattie soup, Rob Hill's Orkney Ale, North Ronaldsay mutton from the famous seaweed eating sheep, oatcakes, bannocks, shortbread, clootie dumpling and 200 hot dropped Scotch pancake scones!

There was much more besides but the ultimate 'jam topping' was an Old Fashioned Orkney Banquet at the family owned Foveran Hotel.

Finally, we paid tribute to our well-loved Daughter of Holm, F. Marian McNeill, whose life and recipes inspired me to create Highland Park Orkney Broonie in her memory. Raising a special glass of 18 year old single malt in salute we drank a toast to her legacy for, as the great lady said, 'We may live without friends, we may live without books, but civilised man cannot live without cooks.'

HIGHLAND PARK OLD ORKNEY BANQUET

Enjoy a taste of Old Orkney cleverly cooked and served Foveran style with more than a hint of
Highland Park a great evening shared together with the ' Best Spirit in the World '

To Begin

ORKNEY SEAFOOD PLATTER
Selection of fresh local seafood served with bere meal blinis Featuring Highland Park 12 Year Old Malt
marinaded Orkney Smoked Salmon

TERRINE OF HIGHLAND PARK marinaded ORKNEY PORK AND WESTRAY RABBIT
With Foveran Apple and thyme Jelly Relish

RED PEPPER AND CHILLI GRIMBISTER CHEESE FRITTERS
with Roasted Vegetable Chutney

ALL SERVED WITH A SELECTION OF ORKNEY BERE AND FLOURY BANNOCKS

To Follow

HOME GROWN SUMMER VEGETABLE BREE with Orkney Grain baps

Main Event

FRESH ORKNEY BERE MEAL PASTA
with herb roasted tomato and home made orkney cream crowdie cheese sauce served with the salad of
Foveran grown rocket leaves

TRILOGY OF NORTH RONALDSAY SEAWEED EATING LAMB
tender loin stuffed with traditional black pudding and slow roasted leg and shoulder served with the
cheese and ale sauce and a sweet potato and Orkney tattie mash

SPECIAL 15 YEAR OLD HIGHLAND PARK MALT WHISKY POACHED ORKNEY
with Birsay salad and Orkney Oatmeal Tatties

And to Finish

FOVERAN OLA DHU DESSERT
A warm luxurious sticky pudding made with Ola Dhu Beer Served

ROASTED RHUBARB AND ORKNEY ARCTIC RASPBERRY
with home-made ice cream

Freshly brewed Tea or Coffe with Home-made fow
12 Year Old Miniature of Highland Park Malt Whisky on th

(Should you have any Special Dietary Requirements please advise a m

Orkney International Science Festival is a celebration of the learning which shapes the present and builds towards a better future. Food heritage plays a role, for by preserving regional culture we retain, sometimes regain, knowledge that will develop resources to enhance future food security. With emphasis on community, visitors dip into and enjoy traditional Orkney fare. Who better to do this than the experienced cooks and bakers of Orkney itself?

BRIE AND CRAB STUFFED PORTOBELLO MUSHROOMS

One of Chef Lorna's fresh Westray crab dishes served at the Lynnfield Hotel.

Serves 4
Takes 20 minutes to prepare and cook
Oven bake at 180C, 350F, Gas 4

You will need:-
4 Portobello mushrooms, stemmed removed and chopped
1 tbsp of melted butter
1 chopped clove of garlic
1tbsp of finely chopped onion
1 tsp Worcester sauce
60g (2ozs) white crab meat
Juice of half a lime
1tbsp of mayonnaise
4 large slices of brie
Sea salt and ground black pepper

To make:-
1. Wash and dry mushrooms, place on a baking tray, brush with butter, and season.
2. Sauté chopped stems, garlic and onion in remaining butter, stir in Worcester sauce.
3. Mix crab meat, mayonnaise and lime juice.
4. Fill mushrooms with mushroom and onion, top with crab and, finally, brie.
5. Bake approximately 10 minutes till tender and cheese has melted.

RED PEPPER AND CHILLI GRIMBISTER FARM CHEESE FRITTERS

Featured in the Highland Park Old Orkney Banquet at the Foveran Hotel.

Serves 6 people
Takes 30 minutes to prepare, this can be done the day before.
Cook on the hob for five minutes.

You will need:-
450g (1lb) red pepper and chilli Grimbister Farm cheese
Thin batter of flour mixed with cold water and a pinch of salt
Fresh brown breadcrumbs
Olive oil

To make:-
1. Cut slices of cheese about 5mm (0.25inch) thick and chill well. Make the batter.
2. Dip the chilled cheese into the batter, then into the breadcrumbs and chill well again till needed.
3. Heat olive oil in a frying pan, cook quickly on both sides till golden.
4. Serve hot with salad leaves to garnish and a pot of your favourite chutney on the side.

HIGHLAND PARK OLA DHU MUFFINS

A centenary tribute to Marjorie Linklater, a stalwart of Orcadian culture, featured this muffin baked with Ola Dhu traditional ale because she was a traditionalist with a view to the future.

Makes 16 to 18 muffins
Takes 45 minutes to prepare and bake
Oven bake at 200C, 400F,
Gas 5 on the middle shelf

You will need:-
1 bottle Highland Park Ola Dhu beer
300g (10ozs) plain flour sifted with 60g (2ozs)
cocoa powder and 1 tbsp baking powder
115g (4ozs) soft brown sugar
60mls (4 tablespoons) sunflower oil
2 eggs
30g (1oz) dark chocolate chips
30g (1oz) white chocolate chips
30g (1ozs) toffee pieces
Milk to mix

To make:-
1. Turn on the oven to heat and prepare baking trays with eighteen muffin cases.
2. Place the sifted flour mix in a bowl, add chocolate and toffee and stir together.
3. Beat eggs, oil and 120mls of beer. Stir into dry ingredients with enough milk to make a soft dropping consistency. Divide between the muffin cases.
4. Bake for fifteen to twenty minutes till risen and firm.
5. Pierce the top of each while warm to make a small tunnel. Drizzle with Ola Dhu.
6. Leave to cool on the tray.

Cook's tip:-
Visit the vet's and buy an equine feed syringe for the princely sum of around 30p. Makes basting and soaking with liquids very simple.

INDEX OF RECIPES

An Orcadian toast to you inspired by the names of two farms on the island of Flotta. Raise a glass to clink, 'Hunger him in', to which the reply is, 'Hunger him out'. For the hunger to come:-
www.lizashworth.co.uk